humoR

for the heart

Stories, Quips, and Quotes
to Lift the Heart

hum♥R
for the heart

Barbara Johnson • Max Lucado
Marilyn Meberg • Chonda Pierce
Dennis Swanberg • Charles Swindoll
and more

HOWARD
PUBLISHING CO.

Our purpose at Howard Publishing is to:
- *Increase faith* in the hearts of growing Christians
- *Inspire holiness* in the lives of believers
- *Instill hope* in the hearts of struggling people everywhere
Because He's coming again!

Humor for the Heart © 2000 by Howard Publishing Co., Inc.
All rights reserved. Printed in the United States of America

Published by Howard Publishing Co., Inc.,
3117 North 7th Street, West Monroe, Louisiana 71291-2227

03 04 05 06 07 08 09   10 9 8 7 6

Library of Congress Cataloging-in-Publication Data
  Humor for the heart : stories, quips, and quotes to lift the heart / compiled by Shari MacDonald ; illustrated by Kristen Myers.
      p. cm.
   ISBN 1-58229-128-4
      1. American wit and humor. I. MacDonald, Shari. II. Myers, Kristen.

PN6162 .H75 2000
818'.60208—dc21   00-063379

Compiled by Shari MacDonald
Cover art by John Luke
Illustrated by Kristen Myers
Interior design by Stephanie Denney

Scripture quotations are from the *New American Standard Bible*, © 1973 by The Lockman Foundation.

Contents

Chapter 1: humoR for the spirit

Chapter 2: the gift of humoR

Chapter 3: humoR on the homefront

Chapter 4: dad—the family comedian

Chapter 5: merriment for moms

Chapter 6: good sports—laughter on the playing field

Chapter 7: viva la difference—humoR between men and women

Contents

Chapter 8: it's my body and i'll cry if i want to—weighty humoR

Chapter 9: the family that laughs together...

Chapter 10: amusing animals—pet humoR

Contents

"There is a time for everything,
and a season for every activity under heaven...
a time to weep
and a time to laugh...."
—Ecclesiastes 3:1, 4

Chapter 1

hum◆R
for the spirit

Hard to Be Good

When I picked up my two boys from their last day of Vacation Bible School, I asked if they would like to attend next summer. "Yes, but I think next year should only be four days," said my 5-year-old. Puzzled, I asked him why.

"Because it's hard to be good five days in a row," he replied.

—FROM "LIFE IN OUR HOUSE," CHRISTIAN PARENTING TODAY (MAY/JUNE 1999)

Hey, Kids, Wanna Ride?

Charles R. Swindoll

Cynthia and I are into Harley-Davidson motorcycles.

I know, I know…it doesn't fit our image. Who really cares? We stopped worrying about our image years ago. We should be ashamed of ourselves? We aren't. We're having a mutual mid-life crisis? We hope so. We should be better examples to the youth? They love it! Actually, it's only a few crotchety adults who don't. What are we going to say to our grandkids? "Hey, kids, wanna ride?" And how are we supposed to explain it to the "the board?" They don't care either.

We are having more fun than anybody can imagine (except fellow Harley riders). One of the best things about the whole deal is that those guys and gals down at the bike shop don't have a clue as to who we are. We have *finally* found a place in our area where we can be out in public and remain absolutely anonymous. If anybody down there happens to ask our names, we'll just tell 'em we're Jim and Shirley Dobson. Those Harley hogs don't know them either.

You should have been in the showroom when I first sat on one of those big bikes. Cynthia stood a few feet away and just stared. She didn't know whether to laugh out loud or witness to me. She compromised and hopped on behind after I winked at her. She couldn't resist. As soon as she leaned forward and whispered in my ear, "Honey, I could get used to this," I knew it wouldn't be long before we'd be truckin' down the asphalt without a worry in the world.

We sat there and giggled like a couple of high school sweethearts sipping a soda through two straws. She liked the feel of sitting close to me (she couldn't resist, naturally), and I liked the feel of her behind me and that giant engine underneath us. And that inimitable Harley *roar*. Man, it was great!

Suddenly, sitting on that shiny black heritage Softail Classic with thick leather saddlebags, we were on the back streets of Houston in 1953 all over again, roaring our way to a Milby High School football game. She was wearing my letterman's sweater and red-and-white saddle oxfords, and I had a flattop with a ducktail and a black leather jacket with fringe and chrome studs!

When we came back to our senses, we realized that somehow we were sorta misfits. I mean, a responsible senior pastor and radio preacher in a suit and tie with a classy, well-dressed woman who is executive vice president of Insight for Living perched on a Harley-Davidson in a motorcycle showroom. Everybody else was wearing t-shirts, torn jeans, boots, black leather stuff, and sported tattoos. I saw one guy who had a tattoo on each arm...one was a snarling bulldog with a spiked collar and the other was a Marine insignia—the eagle, globe, and anchor of the

Corps! A few folks were glancing in our direction as if to say, "Get serious!" And Cynthia leaned up again and whispered, "Do you think we ought to be in here?"

"Of course, honey, who cares? After all, *I'm a Marine!* What I need is a pair of black jeans and leather chaps and all you need is a tattoo, and we'll blend right in." The jeans and chaps for me, probably someday. But Cynthia with a tattoo? I rather doubt it. Somehow I don't think it would go over very big at formal church dinners and the National Religious Broadcasters banquets.

We have had one hilarious time with this in our family. Especially since I raised all four kids with only one unchangeable Swindoll rule: "You will not *ever* ride or own a motorcycle!" Now the old man and his babe are roaring all around town. And it's our now-grown kids who are trying to figure out what's happened to their parents and what to say to *their* kids when they see their grandparents tooling down the freeway like a couple of gray-haired teenagers. Actually, we're getting concerned lately that our children may be a little too strict with *their* kids. "Ya gotta lighten up, guys," as they say down at the Harley hangout. The only one of the bunch who fully understands is our youngest, Chuck—but that makes sense. He rides a Harley too.

What's happening? What would ever possess me to start messing around with a motorcycle, cruising some of the picturesque roads down by the ocean, or taking off with my son for a relaxed, easygoing two or three hours together? What's this all about?

It's about forgetting all the nonsense that every single moment in life is serious. It's about breaking the thick and rigid

"All you need is a tattoo, and we'll blend right in."

mold of predictability. It's about enjoying a completely different slice of life where I don't have to concern myself with living up to anyone else's expectations or worry about who thinks what. It's about being with one of our kids in a world that is totally on his turf (for a change), not mine, in a setting that is just plain fun, no work. It's about being me, nobody else.

It's about breaking the bondage of tunnel vision. It's about refusing to live my life playing one note on one instrument in one room and finding pleasure in a symphony of sounds and sights and smells. It's about widening the radius of a restrictive and demanding schedule where breathing fresh air is sometimes difficult and thinking creative thoughts is occasionally the next thing to impossible.

Bottom line, it's about freedom. That's it, plain and simple. It's about being free.

It's about entering into a tension-free, worry-free world where I don't have to say something profound or fix anyone or do anything other than feel the wind and smell the flowers and hug my wife and laugh till we're hoarse. That's it in a nutshell…it's about freeing ourselves up to laugh again.

In Jesus' day He took His twelve disciples across a lake to enjoy some R&R alone on a mountainside. Who knows what they did for fun? Maybe they climbed rocks or swam in a cool lake or sat around a campfire and told a few jokes. Whatever, you can count on this—they laughed. Today, Cynthia and I prefer to hop on the old Harley. If Jesus lived on earth today, He might ride with us. But something in me says He probably wouldn't get a tattoo. Then again, who knows? He did a lot of other stuff that made the legalists squirm. He knew the truth…and the truth had really set Him free.

You Gotta Hold the Baby Even When She Spits

Chris Fabry

Fistfights break out whenever we bring a baby home for the first time. It happens every time. As soon as Andrea gets in the door with the tightly wrapped child, little voices call out, "I want to hold her! I want to hold her!"

I'm a lot more lenient than I used to be. With our first baby you had to have a graduate degree in child development just to pull the blanket off her face. Now with seven kids, someone at the grocery store will smile and I'll hand the bundle over like a twenty-nine-cent can of pork and beans.

Still, with very tiny hands begging to hold the new one, you have to be careful. There is wisdom in supervising the holding experience. You sit and place a hand under the baby's neck and tell your daughter what a wonderful mommy she will make some day. Secretly you hope to get the baby back with its spinal column intact.

"That's it, sweetie, now hold her snug but not too tight. There you go. Whoops! Ha-ha—not that tight, let's give her a little oxygen now. When she turns those funny colors it means you need to hold her softer. There. Good. Okay, now if you'll put your hand right here behind her head, it won't swing back and forth along the ground. That's it. Good girl!"

Our children have been quick learners, so the following story should not deter you from asking them to baby-sit, should you have the opportunity. In order to protect her identity, I will refer to the offending child as "Sibling."

Sibling wanted to hold the baby when Kaitlyn was only a few weeks old. Kaitlyn was dressed in a pink infant dress, and what little hair she had was coiffured with a matching ribbon. She was adorable. This no doubt added to Sibling's desire of holding such a living doll.

Sibling lovingly cradled little Kaitlyn in her arms and said sweet things to her. I turned my back for a second. The next thing I knew, little Kaitlyn was bouncing on the floor. Thank God for thick carpeting and Stainmaster. I picked her up and calmed her, then looked at her astonished Sibling.

"What happened?" I said.

"She spit on me!" Sibling said, as if this kind of thing never happens.

I helped Sibling clean her own pretty dress and said, "It's important to remember: You gotta hold the baby even when she spits."

She frowned and went into another room, leaving me to ponder my own lesson. Life looks so wonderful from our limited viewpoint. When we're young, it's fluffy and pink and we can't imagine it will taste like anything other than cotton candy. We dream of "what could be," forget "what might be," and take hold with both hands. On the way to "what will be," "what is" starts tasting less like candy and more like Pepto-Bismol. Then life spits up. As it grows older, life spits up *and* kicks us in the teeth, and we're occasionally tempted just to drop the whole thing.

But the more life you live, the more you love it, and even when it's bad you learn to not let go. The spitting and kicking make the other parts that much more enjoyable.

If this is your life, remember that spitting lasts for a season, but joy comes in the morning. That's sort of in the Bible. And if you ever drop the baby, pick it up and hang on. There's a Father who loves you in spite of it all.

Getting Little

Thomas Kinkade

"Daddy, look at me!"

My three-year-old daughter perched proudly atop our big cushioned armchair, her wiry little body poised for another stunt in our "family gymnastics" session. I turned my head just in time to see her turn a perfect somersault from the chair down to the pile of cushions I had placed on the living room floor. Bouncing to her feet like an Olympic gymnast, she treated me with a triumphant smile.

"Boy," I said, "that looks like fun!"

"It is, Daddy!" she enthused. "You do it, too!"

I shook my head, mindful both of the furniture and my not-quite-as-young-as-it-was body. "Better not, honey," I told her. "I'm sort of big for that chair, don't you think?"

She patted me on the shoulder before clambering up for another try.

"It's all right, Daddy," she said encouragingly. "When you get little, you can do it."

I laughed. It was just one of those adorable things that children say. And then, ping!—it hit me. In one of those flashes of insight that often emerge from conversations with little ones, I realized my three-year-old had neatly summarized a vital principle of living in the light.

"When you get little," she said, "you can do it."

She was right.

I thought of the inspiring story from the Bible, often quoted, in which Jesus admonished his followers, "Unless you...become as little children, you will by no means enter the kingdom of heaven." The same reality has been observed and restated by poets and prophets over the centuries. There are some important things about light-filled living that children know but most adults have forgotten.

It's as if, in our determined scramble toward adulthood, we leave some valuable treasures behind us. We would all lead better and brighter lives if, at least now and then, we made a point of "getting little" enough to recover them.

After my three-year-old turned another perfect somersault off that chair, I climbed up, perched myself unsteadily on the same piece of furniture, cast a wary eye on the stack of cushions before me.

Then I took the plunge. I rolled myself forward, managed to tuck my head beneath my shoulders, and landed more or less squarely on the cushions. The furniture was a bit worse for wear, but I was exhilarated.

My daughter was, too.

"You did it, Daddy," she squealed as I pushed to my feet. "I knew you could do it!"

We stood up together and smiled. Two children holding hands.

Remembering What to Forget

Al Sanders

"I know I'm getting older," someone told me recently, "because I keep making mental notes to myself and then forgetting where I put them!"

Another person solved the mental-note problem by writing things down. "Now I write down everything I want to remember," he said. "That way, instead of spending a lot of time trying to remember what I wrote down, I spend the time looking for the paper where I wrote it!"

As we age, we tend to forget things and lose our belongings. As one senior citizen quipped, "Happiness is finding your glasses before you forget *why* you wanted them in the first place." It seems in our later years we more frequently forget names. Then we forget faces. And next we forget...

Sorry! I forgot where I was going with this thought...

Oh yes, forgetfulness!

Do you find yourself having more trouble remembering things as each year passes, often confusing names and details? Well, don't think you're suffering a problem that afflicts only the aged! I don't know the source of the following list, but it supposedly came from a sixth-grade Sunday school class that was surveyed to see how much the youngsters knew about the Bible. Read the answers the students gave, and you may not feel so bad about *your* memory!

- "The first book of the Bible is Guineses, in which Adam and Eve were created from an apple tree."
- "Noah's wife was called Joan of Ark."
- "Samson slayed the Philistines with the ax of the apostles."
- "Unleavened bread is bread made without ingredients."
- "Moses went to the top of My Cyanide to get the 10 Commandments."
- "Joshua led the Hebrews in the battle of Geritol."
- "David fought with the Finkelsteins, a race of people who lived in biblical times."
- "The people who follow Jesus were called the twelve deci-bels."
- "One of the opossums was Saint Matthew."

While it's usually a nuisance, if not an embarrassment, to forget a date or name or fact we really want to remember, forgetting some things isn't bad at all. For example, Paul himself forcefully declared, "One thing I do, forgetting those things which are behind and reaching forward to those things which are ahead, I press toward the goal for the prize of the upward call of God in Christ Jesus" (Philippians 3:13–14).

Paul was reminding us there are things we *should* forget. Unfortunately, those are the things that sometimes seem to

"Joshua led the Hebrews in the battle of Geritol."

stick most tenaciously in our memories! For instance, do you have trouble forgetting an unkind word a person may have said to you? Probably not! Or how about a promise someone has failed to keep? Do you have to work to remember a complaint someone made about your work or your actions?

In marriage it is especially helpful if both husband and wife can forget a few things: hurts for which an apology has been offered and accepted; insignificant irritants that, unless they are forgiven and forgotten, have the potential to make spouses impatient and angry; all the little annoyances that will make absolutely *no* difference when we are called to glory! Actually, once we start thinking about all the inconsequential matters that tend to stick in our minds and make us miserable, we come to agree with Jack Hayford, who says, "We can hardly overestimate the relative unimportance of almost everything!"

Some of us allow remembered *negatives* to become the ruling passion of our lives while, ironically, those who have slighted us have totally forgotten why we are angry at them! Such a situation proves the point that we don't hold grudges—they hold *us,* like an ever-tightening and restrictive vice. Think about this: If God casts *our* sins into the "depths of the sea" (Micah 7:19), He can help us cast our grudges into the vast sea of our forgetfulness. Ask Him to help you heave those heavy burdens right into the ocean. On their way down, they may just knock loose a happy thought you wanted to remember! As it bubbles to the surface, *don't forget* to say, "Thank You, Lord!"

Chapter 2

the gift of hum♥R

Sweet Revenge

When my three-year-old son opened the birthday gift from his grandmother, he discovered a water pistol. He squealed with delight and headed for the nearest sink. I was not so pleased. I turned to Mom and said, "I'm surprised at you. Don't you remember how we used to drive you crazy with water guns?"

Mom smiled and replied..."I remember."

—FROM EFFECTIVE PARENTING,
SCOTT TURANSKY, D. MIN.
AND JOANNE MILLER, R.N., B.S.N.

You Did This for Me?

Max Lucado

He deserves our compassion. When you see him do not laugh. Do not mock. Do not turn away or shake your head. Just gently lead him to the nearest bench and help him sit down.

Have pity on the man. He is so fearful, so wide-eyed. He's a deer on the streets of Manhattan. Tarzan walking through the urban jungle. He's a beached whale, wondering how he got here, and how he'll get out.

Who is this forlorn creature? This ashen-faced orphan? He is—please remove your hats out of respect—he is the man in the women's department. Looking for a gift.

The season may be Christmas. The date may be her birthday or their anniversary. Whatever the motive, he has come out of hiding. Leaving behind his familiar habitat of sporting goods stores, food courts and the big-screen television in the appliance department, he ventures into the unknown world of women's wear. You'll spot him easily. He's the motionless one in the aisle. Were it not for the sweat rings under his arms you'd think he was a mannequin.

But he isn't. He is a man in a woman's world, and he's never seen so much underwear. At the Wal-Mart where he buys his, it's all wrapped up and fits on one shelf. But here he is in a forest of lace. His father warned him about places like this. Though the sign above says "linger-ie," he knows he shouldn't.

So he moves on, but he doesn't know where to go. You see, not every man has been prepared for this moment like I was. My father saw the challenge of shopping for women as a rite of passage, right in there with birds and bees and tying neckties. He taught my brother and me how to survive when we shopped. I can remember the day he sat us down and taught us two words. To get around in a foreign country, you need to know the language, and my father taught us the language of the ladies department.

"There will come a time," he said solemnly, "when a sales person will offer to help you. At that moment take a deep breath and say this phrase, 'Es-tée Lau-der.'" On every gift-giving occasion for years after, my mom received three gifts from the three men in her life: Estée Lauder, Estée Lauder and Estée Lauder.

My fear of the women's department was gone. But then I met Denalyn. Denalyn doesn't like Estée Lauder. Though I told her it made her smell motherly, she didn't change her mind. I've been in a bind ever since.

This year for her birthday I opted to buy her a dress. When the salesperson asked me Denalyn's size, I said I didn't know. I honestly don't. I know I can wrap my arm around her, and that her hand fits nicely in mine. But her dress size? I never inquired. There are certain questions a man doesn't ask.

The woman tried to be helpful. "How does she compare to me?" Now, I was taught to be polite to women, but I couldn't be polite and answer that question. There was only one answer, "She is thinner."

I stared at my feet, looking for a reply. After all, I write books. Surely I can think of the right words.

I considered being direct: "She is less of you."

Or complimentary. "You are more of a woman than she is."

Perhaps a hint would suffice? "I hear the company is *downsizing.*"

Finally, I swallowed and said the only thing I knew to say, "Estée Lauder?"

She pointed me in the direction of the perfume department, but I knew better than to enter. I would try the purses. Thought it would be easy. What could be complicated about selecting a tool for holding cards and money? I've used the same money clip for eight years. What would be difficult about buying a purse?

Oh, naive soul that I am. Tell an attendant in the men's department that you want a wallet, and you're taken to a small counter next to the cash register. Your only decision is black or brown. Tell an attendant in the ladies department that you want a purse, and you are escorted to a room. A room of shelves. Shelves with purses. Purses with price tags. Small but potent price tags...prices so potent that they should remove the need for a purse, right?

I was taught to be polite to women, but I couldn't be polite and answer that question.

I was pondering this thought when the salesperson asked me some questions. Questions for which I had no answer. "What kind of purse would your wife like?" My blank look told her I was clueless, so she began listing the options: "Handbag? Shoulder bag? Glove bag? Back pack? Shoulder pack? Change purse?"

Dizzied by the number of options, I had to sit down and put my head between my knees lest I faint. Didn't stop her. Leaning over me she continued, "Moneybag? Tote-bag? Pocketbook? Satchel?"

"Satchel?" I perked up at the sound of a familiar word. Satchel Paige pitched in the major leagues. This must be the answer. I straightened my shoulders and said proudly, "Satchel."

Apparently she didn't like my answer. She began to curse at me in a foreign language. Forgive me for relating her vulgarity, but she was very crude. I didn't understand all she said, but I do know she called me a "Dooney Bird" and threatened to "brighten" me with a spade that belonged to someone named Kate. When she laid claim to "our mawny," I put my hand over the wallet in my hip pocket and defied, "No, it's my money." That was enough. I got out of there as fast as I could. But as I left the room, I gave her a bit of her own medicine, "Estée Lauder!" I shouted and ran as fast as I could.

Oh, the things we do to give gifts to those we love.

But we don't mind, do we? We would do it all again. Fact is, we do it all again. Every Christmas, every birthday, every so often we find ourselves in foreign territory. Grownups are in toy stores. Dads are in teen stores. Wives are in the hunting department, and husbands are in the purse department.

Not only do we enter unusual places, we do unusual things. We assemble bicycles at midnight. We hide the new tires with mag wheels under the stairs. One fellow I heard about rented a movie theater so that he and his wife could see their wedding pictures on their anniversary.

And we'd do it all again. Having pressed the grapes of service, we drink life's sweetest wine—the wine of giving. We are at our best when we are giving. In fact, we are most like God when we are giving.

H♥w to Buy Gifts f♥r Dummies

Chonda Pierce

When I go to the bookstore and see all those bright yellow books that take up a whole wall, I can't help but feel like such a dummy. I look at some of the titles and think, "I could sure use that." At first I thought the publisher had a really cute idea: Take something complicated (like building a lunar space probe) and explain it in layman's terms. But just the other day I saw *Gardening for Dummies, Fishing for Dummies, Pregnancy for Dummies, Crossword Puzzles for Dummies, Bowling for Dummies,* and even *Beauty Secrets for Dummies.*

I've always been too embarrassed to buy any of these for myself. I was afraid the cashier would snicker. So for a while I tried to stay away from bookstores, but that's almost impossible when your husband is an English professor and makes a living reading and writing books.

Then one day, while standing by the bright yellow rows that

he so lovingly refers to as "Chonda's own personal reference section" (I didn't laugh), I had this great idea. If I didn't have the nerve to buy them for myself, I should buy these books for people who really needed help more than I did. It would be like finding a Bible verse that I knew someone else really needed to hear—like my husband. So, in a way, buying these books and then giving them away to those in need would be like a ministry. (Isn't it funny how far our minds will go to justify our actions?)

The first book I bought was for my husband.

"A present for me?" he said, pleasantly surprised. He tore open the package to reveal a bright yellow book entitled *Putting the Toilet Seat Down for Dummies.* It was handsomely done with graphs, charts, and illustrations, and David spent a great deal of that evening reading and studying. Every now and then I'd hear him make one of those "Ooh!" sounds of discovery, and he would dog-ear a page so he could find it quickly later. For the next few weeks, I couldn't have been more pleased with the results.

The next book I bought was for our neighbors down the road. It was entitled *Walking Your Dog for Dummies.* I even bought a bookmark with a picture of a cute dog with floppy ears and stuck it in at the beginning of chapter four: "Keeping Your Dog from Relieving Itself in Other People's Front Yards." I wrapped the book up nicely in old newspaper (nothing wrong with just a little hint) and left it on their front porch.

One of the most worthwhile purchases I made was *Making Change for Dummies.* I gave it to the cashier at Kroger's who takes forever to give me my money back, especially if I give

If I didn't have the nerve to buy them for myself, I should buy these books for people who really needed help more than I did.

him an extra penny to round off the amount, thinking it will make his job easier. After only a few weeks, the book paid for itself in my time alone.

I almost tripped all over myself when I found *Preaching for Dummies*. I bought two of them (one for my associate pastor, too). This one was chock-full of great chapters like "Ending a Sermon on Time, Part I," "How to Take Up an Offering Without Sounding Like You're Begging," "How to Take Up an Offering Every Time You Get Together Without Everyone Thinking You're Taking Up an Offering Every Time You Get Together," and my favorite, "Ending a Sermon on Time, Part II." I can't wait until Pastor Appreciation Sunday!

Since I first discovered the value of these books (and how most everyone will benefit from this kindness), I've given away dozens—a small price to pay to change someone's life. I bought *Picking Up Garbage for Dummies* for our garbage collector (mainly for the chapters "How to Keep the Can Standing Upright after You've Dumped the *Entire* Contents into the Back of the Truck" and "What to Do When Some of It Falls onto the Customer's Yard"). I went ahead and bought a couple dozen *Using Your Turn Signal for Dummies* and left a stack of them on the counter at our local Golden Gallon gas station, telling the cashier to give them away to whomever he thought could use one. (I also saved one of those for Mom, only because they haven't yet published *Turning Your Turn Signal Off for Dummies*, but I'm watching.) I gave my brother a copy of *Getting Along with Your Little Sister for Dummies* since we have a family reunion just around the corner.

I was buying books right and left and was starting to think that the world *could* be a better place. I even grew bold enough to

buy a book for me: *Making the World a Better Place for Dummies.*
Yes, what an exciting new ministry. Everyone around me seemed
to be growing and maturing, and sometimes I could just sit and
watch them become better people, like watching a rosebud open
into a beautiful bloom.

Then one day I received a package in the mail with no return
address. I opened it and found one of those bright yellow books,
one I hadn't seen before:

Minding Your Own Business for Dummies.

The Gift
Nancy Moser

Six children, six years old. Boys. At a birthday party. Excedrin headache #85.

But I was smart. I'd moved the festivities from home sweet home to the local Mexican restaurant that specialized in such things. Why any business would willingly invite gaggles of birthday-crazed children into their establishment to spill drinks, topple chairs, and cover the floor with crumbs was beyond me. But if they were willing, I'd comply—whatever the price. Better their floor than mine.

The Party Coordinator was young (a prerequisite) and enthusiastic (give her time). She herded the boys into a far corner of the restaurant that was marked with balloons tied onto every chair—a warning to other diners: *Stay back! Way back!* As the boys scrambled onto the chairs (knocking two out of the six to the ground) she handed out party hats, including a huge sombrero for Carson, the birthday boy.

I took my camera position a safe distance away, and let her do her stuff.

Pin the tail on the donkey. Bean bag toss. Word scramble (TSROBRUI = BURRITOS). Untied shoelaces, runny noses, bobbing cowlicks.

It was time to open the gifts. The boys sat on their knees and leaned across the table, anxious for Carson to "Open mine first!"

It was then I noticed that one boy, Matthew, was sitting quietly in his chair. He stuffed his hands into the pockets of his down vest. His eyes flitted between Carson and the front door of the restaurant. His legs dangled with a rhythm that quickened with each passing minute.

Paper was ripped. Bows were squashed. One present opened. Two.

Matthew wiggled in his chair. His head jerked toward the door as customers left and others entered. He bit his lip.

What was wrong?

It had something to do with the presents. I counted them. Five guests...four presents.

Matthew didn't have a present to give Carson! I gave an inward sigh. How could I let him know it didn't matter? How could I tell—

Matthew stood. All the presents had been opened—except his.

It's OK, Matthew. You don't need—

Matthew pulled a dog-chewed plastic figure of a soldier out of the pocket of his vest. He handed it to Carson.

"Happy birthday," he said.

I prayed my six-year-old would show some etiquette far beyond his years.

"Thanks, Matthew," Carson said.

Good boy.

"Matthew?"

Matthew's head snapped toward the voice of his mother. She had come in the restaurant unnoticed. She handed him a beautifully wrapped birthday present for Carson.

The look on Matthew's face was worth a hundred gifts. A thousand. His fidgeting stopped. His shoulders straightened as he handed Carson the gift.

"Happy birthday, Carson," he said again.

Carson opened the present.

"Thanks, Matthew," he said. "Thanks for both presents."

Matthew's mother looked puzzled. While the boys were eating their cake and spilling their juice, I let her in on the secret.

I told her about her son's gift of the toy soldier.

Her eyes filled with proud tears. As did mine. We felt honored to have witnessed true giving. From a six-year-old boy. A grimy-faced, scraped-knees, heaven-sent little boy.

A boy who had given all that he had.

Fl♥wers and Weeds
Philip Gulley

Once a year my wife has a birthday. It's been that way as long as I've known her. Every year it's the same problem—what do you get the woman who has everything? Most of the time I buy her jewelry. One time I gave her a bracelet. She told me it was so beautiful she'd hate to lose it. So she put it in her jewelry box, where it's been ever since. It's still in perfect condition. She's taken fine care of it.

I decided one year to give her something she could use. Our iron was making funny noises on the steam setting, so I thought I would buy her a new iron. I asked my sister her opinion. She told me not to buy Joan an iron, that it wasn't very romantic. I'm glad I listened to my sister. Irons aren't very romantic. It would be like giving someone a vacuum cleaner. The boys and I went to Furrow's Hardware and bought her a wheelbarrow instead.

The week before, Joan and the boys had been outside cleaning up the yard, picking up sticks and putting them in the wheelbarrow. The load was unbalanced, and the wheelbarrow kept tipping over whenever Joan pushed it. So I bought her a wheelbarrow with two wheels. I don't mean to boast, but that kind of thoughtful consideration has enabled our marriage to flourish.

Whenever Joan works in the yard, she takes the boys with her. She's teaching them the difference between weeds and flowers. They're not in school yet, but they can already distinguish between wild bloodwort and shepherd's purse. Joan wants them to know these things before they're turned loose to hoe the flower beds. Though it isn't an easy lesson to teach, it's an important one to learn. Otherwise, they'll spend their lives confusing weeds for flowers and flowers for weeds.

Buying my wife a new wheelbarrow raised the problem of what to do with the old one. The tire had a slow leak. Every time we used it, we had to pump up the tire. If we used it more than an hour, we had to put more air in it. It's been like that all ten years we've owned it, a burden from day one. I filled the tire, hosed off the wheelbarrow, hung a *Free* sign on it, and hauled it to the curb.

A man down the street spied it, shiny and red, glistening in the sun, tire full. He wheeled it across the street to his yard, delighted with his unexpected find. I drove by his house later that day. He was pushing the wheelbarrow across his yard. It was full of sticks; the tire was flat. It tipped over and the sticks fell out. He began kicking the wheelbarrow. I could hear him cuss and swear. Ordinarily, he is a saintly man, but that wheelbarrow has tarnished many a halo.

This man has been living under a burden since the day he took up with that wheelbarrow. One falling domino after another. Because he didn't pick up the sticks, he rolled over a limb and broke his mower. While he was shopping for a new one, the dandelions moved in and took over. He ended up having to spray his entire yard. I was going to offer my help, but by then he wasn't speaking to me. All of this from a wheelbarrow marked *Free*.

We take some things into our lives which have a veneer of blessing, and they exact a price we can scarcely imagine. We confuse bane for blessing and blessing for bane. I watch Joan teach our sons the difference between flower and weed. I hope it will be a primer for their later years, that those garden lessons will be their start in lives of wise discernment. I hope they'll learn that just because something's sitting at the curb marked *Free*, doesn't mean it really is.

Jesus once taught about how the cares of the world can grind a plant down to nothing. These "cares" are the things we bring into our lives with scarcely a thought. They promise good and deliver ill—the material goods that enslave us, the relationships that crush our spirits, the careers that tax our souls. Most of us have a flat-tired wheelbarrow haunting us one way or another. It helps to learn the difference between weeds and flowers, whether something should be left sitting at the curb or carried home with joy.

Chapter 3

humⓥR
on the homefront

Ways to Know if
Martha Stewart Is Stalking You

- You find a lemon slice in the dog's water bowl.

- You discover that every napkin in the entire house has been folded into a swan.

- No matter where you eat, your place setting always includes an oyster fork.

- You wake up in the hospital with a concussion and endive stuffing in both ears.

- You awaken one morning with a glue gun pointed squarely at your temple.

—FROM CHOCOLATE CHILI PEPPER LOVE, BECKY FREEMAN

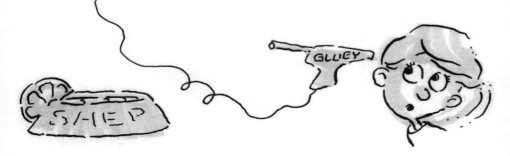

Encroaching the Throne

G. Ron Darbee

Home! I threw the gearshift forward, set the parking brake, and removed my key from the ignition. Slowly, carefully, I turned my head to the side and surveyed the fifteen feet or so separating me from the sanctity of my front door. I could make it. Maybe not with style, and certainly a little shy of pizzazz, but with a fair amount of effort, I could pick up my briefcase and drag what remained of Ron Darbee up the sidewalk and into my quiet, peaceful home. Friday—I love Fridays.

I opened the car door and swung out first one leg, then another, and using the armrest for balance, pushed my tired frame to a modified standing position. *Forget the briefcase,* I thought. *It will be there on Monday when I start this routine all over again.*

I took the fifteen-foot hike in slow and methodical fashion. It felt as if I carried the entire defensive line of the New York Giants on my shoulders. The old Giants, back when Lawrence Taylor ate quarterbacks for breakfast and all was well in football. But I knew I would cross the goal line. I had vision. I had purpose. My chair awaited me.

Our home is full of chairs: desk chairs, kitchen chairs, chairs in the bedroom and in the garage, chairs that rock and chairs that recline, wooden chairs, beanbag chairs, high-chairs, and folding chairs. If there's a chair for the job, we probably own a set. But there is only one chair I call my own.

Like my father before me and his father before him, I have a designated retreat positioned strategically in front of the television. It is the Remote Control Command Center, recliner extraordinaire, a haven for the weary father, my own private, personal throne. It is where I make decisions and take naps. It is the seat from which I read *The Little Engine That Could* to my children and explained the birds-and-the-bees. Report cards come directly to this chair, as do letters addressed, "To the Parents of…" and problems that require Dad's attention.

I know my chair, and it knows me. Every broken spring holds a story. Every creak and groan of the mechanism sounds like music to my ears. It no longer looks like it did in the showroom, but I don't mind because it belongs to me. Of that there has been no question—at least not until recently.

I made it to the door that Friday, into the entryway, and kitchen. It was when I turned the corner that I noticed something was amiss. I saw a pair of sneakers through the door-way, two feet off the ground and where my own belonged. They were the shoes of a usurper, a pretender to the throne.

"Comfortable?" I asked the reclining shape that belonged to my son.

Like my father before me and his father before him, I have a designated retreat positioned strategically in front of the television.

"Yup."

"Can I get you anything? Maybe a soda or some pretzels? I think there are cookies in the cupboard."

"Nope, I'm fine," he answered. "But it's really nice of you to ask." His sister sat on the couch across the room, surveying the situation and taking a few mental notes.

"Well," I continued, "I think a young man should be as comfortable as possible during his last few moments on earth."

"Do you mean me?" he asked. "I'm not going anywhere." He wore a smile—half grin, half smirk—and it was obvious he intended to put up a fight.

"Move it or lose it," I said in that Robert Young, *Father Knows Best,* sort of way.

"Nope."

"OK," I said, "last chance. Get thy mangy backside out of my chair, Goatboy, or suffer your father's wrath."

"O-o-o-h-h-h-h, I'm really scared."

I could see this tack wasn't working and settled on another course. "Come on, Ron, please," I pleaded. "Your Dad is really tired. All I want to do is sit down for a while and relax."

"Plenty of room over there on the nice, comfortable couch," he said, pointing in the direction of his sister. "Feel free to take all the room you want." Melissa, sensing her time had come to join in the festivities, spread herself flat, taking up as much room as her thirteen-year-old body could manage.

"I'm sitting here," she announced with a giggle.

"OK," I said, "I didn't want to do this, but you forced me. "Sue!" I yelled, calling to their mother for assistance. "Your kids won't let me have my chair."

"Poor baby," she said, mock sympathy in her voice, and turning

to the children, "Let your poor old daddy have his chair, before he starts to cry."

"Who said anything about crying?" I questioned. "I only
solicited your help to save our children from the pain and
embarrassment of their father demonstrating his physical su-
periority. Actually," I continued, "I planned to throw
Goatboy for distance and was concerned his Royal Girthness
might land on Melissa, crushing her and rendering her inca-
pable of performing household chores."

"Are those tears I see forming?" Sue asked, now solidifying
her position in the enemy camp. A chorus of "Daddy's crying,
Daddy's crying" rose up from my offspring, and I realized that
somewhere along the way I had lost control.

"All right. All right, fine," I said. "Have a little fun at my
expense. I'll go in the backyard and lie in my hammock."

"Oh, let your father have his chair, Ron," Sue said to our
son. "They don't have much time left together. I suppose we
ought to let him say good-bye."

"Good-bye?" I queried. "What's this about good-bye?"

"The income tax refund came in today's mail," Sue said.
"We agreed we'd buy new furniture for the living room."

"The chair's not furniture," I said. "It's…it's my chair!"

"You act like it's one of the children," Sue said.

"Not at all. That chair never talks back to me. The chair's
loyal and comfortable and dependable."

"D-a-a-a-a-d!" Melissa yelled.

"Quiet, Sweetheart. Your mother and I are talking."

"We agreed," Sue reminded me.

"Not really," I countered. "You were unclear when we dis-
cussed this. You didn't specifically mention my recliner. I

agreed under false pretenses—under duress. That's it; I agreed under duress. Your argument will never hold up in court."

"Are you through yet?"

"That depends, do you still plan on replacing my chair?"

"It's old and worn out," Sue argued. "The entire right side leans out at an angle. How many times have you lost the remote down there?"

"And is that my fate, as well?" I asked. "When I'm old and worn out, when I lean to one side, then will you get rid of me too?"

"You're still here, aren't you?"

"OK, then, Sue. If my chair goes, so does the coffee table and both end tables. How do you like those apples?"

"It's a deal. I'll call Good Will tomorrow."

Sometimes I fear I'm not the sharpest pencil in the box. This feeling usually overcomes me shortly after I open my mouth.

We browsed through nearly every furniture store in the northern San Joaquin valley the next day, and while Sue found tables, a couch, and several other items she was perfectly happy with, I didn't see one suitable chair. Some were too big, others too small. A scarce few of the chairs reclined to the optimum angle, and none felt as comfortable as my personal throne. Several even boasted a few hi-tech extras like adjustable lumbar, built-in cup holders, and holsters for multiple remote controls. Let them keep their vibrating massage and heat control. I wanted my chair.

The drive home could have been more pleasant. Sue called me "picky" and accused me of intentionally finding fault with every La-Z-Boy® that came my way. Of course, I told her she was being ridiculous, but it didn't help. It looked as if we were in for a cold and quiet evening. But then I got an idea.

I pulled the car to the side of the road and began presenting my idea, first in the form of a question. "What's the first rule for a happy marriage?" I asked.

"What are you talking about?"

"Come on, the first rule. What is it?"

"Don't leave your dirty underwear on the floor by the bed?" Sue guessed.

"No, come on. I'm serious."

"This isn't going to be an 'honor your husband' lecture is it?" Sue asked.

"Nothing like that," I said. *"Compromise* is the answer. Marriage requires compromise."

"And what's your idea of compromise? Do we keep all of the old furniture?"

"No," I said, "we reupholster the chair. You can pick the fabric to match the new couch, I'll have all the springs resprung and the side bolted back into place. My chair will look like new and, best of all, it will still be my chair. Come on, Sweetheart, what do you think?"

"It might work," she said. "We can have it restuffed and re-shaped." She paused for a moment to ponder the perceived pluses and minuses of the situation. "Mr. Darbee, you've got yourself a deal." She offered her hand to seal our agreement.

"Thank you, Mrs. Darbee. It's been a pleasure doing business with you."

My chair and I are very happy. It maintains the favored spot in front of our television and remains the Remote Control Command Center, a place from which I can still dispense wisdom. I didn't have the heart to show Sue the bill from the upholstery shop. We could have bought two chairs for the price, but compromise is healthy for a marriage—everybody wins, and nobody loses. Who knows, we may have opportunity to try it again sometime.

"Honey, I'm home!" I yelled, slamming the front door behind me. I set my briefcase down and made a beeline for the living room. Once again, I saw feet breaking the plane of the doorway.

"Move it or lose it, Goat—" I cut myself off in mid sentence. "Sue, why are you in my chair?"

"*Our* chair," she said.

I think I see another compromise on the horizon.

Cleanliness Is Next to Godliness

Karen Scalf Linamen

If cleanliness is next to godliness, then I may be in peril of losing my salvation.

The truth is that I am severely organizationally disadvantaged. It's not that I don't clean my house—indeed, I work hard at it. But even though I work *hard,* I am coming to the conclusion that I must not work *smart.* This is because, at any given moment, you'd be lucky to find one or maybe two rooms in my house that could be considered "company ready." On special occasions when I am, indeed, preparing for company, I might have as many as four rooms in tip-top shape. (Of course, the impact of this accomplishment wanes a little when you think about the fact that, counting bathrooms, I live in an eleven-room house.)

I wish that family life and housework were not so irrevocably linked. Unfortunately, if you have a family, you've got to have a place to put them. That means some sort of abode. And that means housework. Lately I've been pondering the injustice of the fact that I have to spend so many of my waking hours doing something at which I have so little skill. It seems to me that in most situations, if you get stuck with a job for which you have absolutely no aptitude, something eventually happens to save you. It's called getting canned. Sooner or later, someone who collects a bigger salary than you will call you into his office and point out the fact that you are a failure. He will then relieve you of your duties (and your paycheck). This is what happens in the real world. It's actually a good system.

When it comes to housekeeping, I am a failure. But no one ever relieves me of my duties. And there is no paycheck.

This is NOT a good system.

It's not that I'm not worthy of being fired. I mean, think about it: Pretend with me for a moment that you have hired a woman to cook for your family. This woman cooks in such a way that she uses the smoke alarm interchangeably with the oven timer. Let's pretend that last week she was browning hamburger when the smoke alarm began to squeal. Undaunted, she stirred the hamburger, turned on the exhaust fan, and left to set the table. The alarm continued to squeal, which was annoying although not altogether unusual just prior to mealtimes. It wasn't until she ambled back past the stove several minutes later that she noticed a dish towel on fire next to the hamburger.

You would relieve this woman of her duties, wouldn't you? Of course you would. I would, too. Unfortunately, Larry merely suggested that I try to be more careful next time.

What's the world coming to? Doesn't anybody have any standards anymore?

I would also fire a housekeeper who mixed the laundry and sent my husband to work wearing pink underwear.

I would fire any live-in who forgot to buy milk so often that my kids began to believe that Cheerios are actually *supposed* to be consumed with Cremora.

I would fire any domestic help who believed that one way to keep ants from attacking dirty dishes left overnight in the sink is to spray the kitchen counter with Raid (for the complete, unabridged confession on this one, see page 41 of my book *Working Women, Workable Lives*).

And yet no one fires me.

It's just not fair.

I would love to have a clean house. I would love to live in an environment…

…where dust bunnies don't double as the family mascot;

…where refrigerator leftovers don't stick around so long they start getting their own junk mail;

…where I could allow guests to roam free without wondering if they're peeking in my closets and worrying about lawsuits should they happen to become buried under the inevitable resulting avalanche.

Thank God that the condition of my house does not determine the condition of my soul.

P♥tty Talk for the R♥mantically Inclined

Charlene Ann Baumbich

It was time to redecorate the downstairs bathroom. Actually, it was time to redecorate the entire house, but what we could afford in both money and patience was this four-by-four room. The 60s look just didn't cut it.

"New wallpaper?" George asked.

"No, I want to paint it the same color as the living room. I might put a border around the middle, or the top, or both. We'll see."

"Okay. I'll start stripping the old stuff, then I'll paint. Be done with it in no time."

"No, George. Yes, I want to paint, but I also want a new sink and toilet and medicine cabinet and light fixture and towel bar and tissue holder and matching garbage can."

"What's wrong with our old toilet? It still gets the job done."

"It's yellow and I don't want to decorate around it again. I'm sick of yellow. I don't look good in yellow. Yellow makes me look pale. I'd like this bathroom to match the downstairs for a change."

We shopped here and there and everywhere, educating ourselves to possibilities that fit our budget. We couldn't believe the choices and also how much vanities, sinks, and toilets cost! We'd never had to buy a toilet before, and we were stunned. I mean, come on, all it does is flush.

But how do you want it to flush? Button? Handle? Chrome or goldtone? And in what shape do you want the bowl? Round? Elongated?

Basically, we wanted one just like our old one, just not yellow. That, however, was not a possibility. Using nigh on three gallons to flush is no longer politically or environmentally correct. One-point-five gallons. That's all you get to flush your stuff, so it better be do-able. But locating the right toilet was only half the trouble.

Our old vanity no longer came in that same size with a drawer. I needed a drawer! You just can't organize anything without a drawer. After shopping for weeks, I learned that my drawered vanity was an impossible dream unless we went one size larger. "I'm sure that will fit, George, and it has two drawers!"

After endless hours of thrashing and banging and wrestling the new vanity, George emerged from the bathroom and announced that no matter *how* he moved it, he and this size vanity were not going to fit in that bathroom. It was too big, he declared. It would have to go. But I'll never really know because we couldn't both fit in the bathroom at the same time for me to check it myself.

We distracted ourselves by returning the vanity and getting back on the toilet trail until we couldn't stand that anymore and decided to give it all a rest for awhile.

Lickety split, Valentine's Day rolled around, and George took me out for a nice dinner at a nearby restaurant. When the waitress asked if we'd like dessert, I opened my mouth to say yes, and George said, "Let's go look at toilets instead." Ah, romance.

I browsed in the vanity section. When I came around the corner of the aisle, I stopped dead in my tracks.

There was my Valentine, halfway down the aisle, knee to the ground, arm submerged up to his shoulder in a toilet bowl. He went from one toilet to the next, methodically making his way to the end of the row, cramming his arm into each one.

It just doesn't get much better than this.

"What are you doing?" I shouted more than asked. And truly, I didn't want to know. I disappeared around the end of the aisle trying to imagine what was in his mind. Was he trying to figure out where the stuff goes? What?

As it turns out, that is precisely what he was doing. Exactly how big is the space that a mere one-point-five gallons has to flush without plugging up while making its way around all those loop-the-loops? Important. Very important. My hero, the engineer.

Just when I thought the worst was behind us, the round vs. elongated dilemma resurfaced.

"What have we had, George?"

"I don't know."

There was my Valentine, knee to the ground, arm submerged up to his shoulder in a toilet bowl.

"Well, did it look like either one of these? I don't think it did."

"We'll have to go home and see."

"George, I don't want to have to come back here *again.*"

He studied my face for a moment and realized that if he asked me to come back again, he was flirting with a major attack of woe.

"We could just sit on them," I said, "and discover for ourselves. I'm sure our bottoms will recognize a good fit."

George made that snort sound he makes with his nose, but looked as though he might go along with the idea.

Putting all vanity aside, I sat my way down the row; as did George. Date night with the Baumbichs! We nearly cheered when the selection and purchase were made. (We're roundies, in case you're wondering.) We could barely wait to install our new white beauty.

And can you imagine the thrill of flushing that puppy for the first time? We were nearly breathless as George pushed our chrome-choice handle.

No more swirling and twirling. No more spinning and rising and tornadoing its way down the tube. Whoosh! That's what you get when you're politically and environmentally correct.

So stop by and see our beautiful white appliance (for lack of a better word) and blue rug with the matching tank top and purple tissue box and garbage can and liquid soap pump with matching purple guest towel. All I need now is to frame the picture I've selected and shop for the border.

Oh, if you stop by and we're not home, it's because we've decided to redecorate the upstairs bathroom. You can probably find us in aisle seven. That would be us, lounging in the tubs to see how they fit.

Kitchen Hall of Fame

Marti Attoun

I never thought I'd get to say this: I wore out an electric skillet. Took me eight years, but I actually flipped enough burgers and scraped up enough black pancakes to permanently disable the appliance.

This is exciting stuff. It's the first time I've used up a kitchen tool or housekeeping gadget other than a coffee pot. I've gone through a dozen of those, but that doesn't earn me a kitchen badge of courage.

On the night the skillet died, I gathered the family at the trash can for one final viewing. I pointed with pride to the skillet's ragged non-stick surface. I kept the cord as a memory.

"Aren't you being a bit melodramatic?" my husband asked as I recited some of the fine queasine, as he calls it, that the skillet has yielded over the years.

Too dramatic? I don't think so. He has no idea what a burden it's been growing up in the shadow of a woman who's worn out two waffle irons. Finally, it's my turn for glory.

All these years, I've watched my mother snap on one new mop head after another. She finally quit buying replacements and began doubling old towels and clamping them on the mop stick. Mom had good training; her mother wore a hole all the way through a washboard.

My mother has used cookie sheets until they developed permanent flips. She's worn finger grooves in her wooden-handled potato masher.

One of my sisters wore a broom down to its last straw. In awe, I pointed out one day that she was sweeping with little more than a whisker.

"Yes. I keep forgetting to buy another broom," she sighed.

"Frame it," I told her. "This is incredible. I've never met a woman who actually wore out a broom."

She looked at me. "Three of them, actually."

My aunt buys vacuum cleaners repeatedly. She keeps a backup in case her latest one blows.

I still have the mop and broom and cake pan that I bought when I was single and moved into my first apartment. I assumed they'd be heirlooms for my kids.

I've always pictured my kitchen wares being sold in flat little boxes at an estate sale. The auctioneer would hold up my electric skillet and yell to the crowd, "Skillet's like new, folks. Doesn't look like it was ever used. Who'll give me $5?"

Hey, give me five. I wore out an electric skillet.

Chapter 4

dad—
the family
comedian

Bedtime Prayer

Parents know how bedtime prayers can be full of surprises. One little lad, smarting after punishment, finished his prayers with the usual blessings for all the members of the family save one. Then turning to his father he said, "I suppose you noticed you were not included."

—FROM MORE HOLY WIT, JAMES A. SIMPSON

Of Fathers and Children
Tim Wildmon

I have always been interested in the parallel between the parent-child relationship and God's relationship with us, His children. I became increasingly aware of how the Lord may see us sometimes when my first child, Wriley Hope, turned two years old.

Long before she had reached that age, Alison and I decided that we would refer to this one year in Wriley's life as the "terrific twos." All we had ever heard about was the "terrible twos" and we in our inexperience and ignorance thought that the twos couldn't be that big a deal. However, we have since recanted the "terrific twos" statement and realized how very naive we were to expect the twos to be terrific. There's a reason the term "terrible twos" has been around since little Cain and Abel roamed the earth. And positive thinking can only deal with so much reality until it cries uncle.

This all came home to me after a five-minute experience in the convenience store with Wriley. I must say that I suspect my daughter was atypical. Whereas the normally aggressive child is a type A personality, Wriley Hope was an AAA. Like that irritating little bunny on the battery commercial that makes us all want to shoot our television sets, she kept going, and going, and going. And then going some more. She's changed some since then, praise be to God, but at the time Alison and I considered having her tested for whatever it is they test children for who behave as she did. Maybe she had Attention Shoppers Disorder or whatever they call it? We didn't know what to call it besides, "Wriley, bad girl."

One evening, the whole family drove to the convenience store, and Wriley in a half-asking, half-demanding sort of way let it be known that she wanted to go in the store with me. *No problem,* I thought. Quick in, quick out. We made our way through the door and toward the aisle to get some baby food for her nine-month-old brother Wesley. Wriley held my hand sweetly and behaved very well until she saw what I call Candy Row. This area of the store has a magnetic pull on children. With all its vibrant color, the candy wrapping is most appealing to the eye and, with all the sugar, the contents inside the wrapping are most appealing to the taste buds of most folks. Especially small children.

Immediately, upon seeing Sugar City, she shook my hand loose and went to the candy. (At this point, I discovered that it is futile to try to talk with a child about the lust of the flesh or self-control.) *Let her look, what's the harm?* I thought. I also quickly reasoned that I could go ahead and get the baby food and dash back to Wriley before any real damage was done. I was only one row over, after all.

"Okay, let's see here, banana food jar, banana food jar, where's b-a-n-a-n-a?…Banana, banana, banana, where is the stupid banana jar?" I said to myself. "Okay, find the banana jar, Tim! Come on, buddy. For once, go in a store, and come through for your family, son." (Sometimes, I take on the duel roles of father and son when I'm in a testosterone-testing situation such as this.) Alison—who was waiting in the car with Wesley—had told me specifically, twice, to get banana food. She even looked me in the eye just before I closed the door— as she often does—and said, "B-A-N-A-N-A, Tim. It's not hard."

"It's not here," I thought aloud in frustration. "I'm looking directly at the fruit section, and it's not anywhere in sight. We've got your apricot, pineapple, peach, every kind of fruit known to man including gordash—what's gordash?— but this is my luck, there's no b-a-n-a-n-a here."

I almost grabbed two other customers by the arm as they came down the aisle. "Excuse me, do you see any banana food on this shelf anywhere? Five bucks says you can't find any. Go ahead, look. No really, I've got Abe Lincoln right here."

Why me? Why here? Why now? I thought. As soon as I go out to the car and tell Al there's no b-a-n-a-n-a, she'll walk right in here, whereupon the evil and scheming little beady-eyed clerk will have quickly placed several banana jars on the shelf and Alison will find them and she'll give me that "once again you're not paying attention look," sigh, and walk to the counter holding Wesley in one arm, Wriley by the hand, and her purse in her secret third arm (I swear she's got four). Then she'll tell me to go get in the car in front of several

Sometimes, I take on the duel roles of father and son when I'm in a testosterone-testing situation such as this.

other men, I'll go out to the car, pull on the door handle twice, only to remember she has the keys to the locked car. But I don't dare go back in. I'll just stand there by my car door, say "how you doin'" and "nice to see ya" to the folks that walk by and look stupid. For those scoring at home, we have shot par here, ladies and gentlemen.

That, my friends, is a lot to think about. Which is probably why I couldn't find the b-a-n-a-n-a fruit jar in the first place. All this stress is too much for an American male trying to keep up with who's going to win the National League's Eastern division. But I'm not one to make excuses. Very often anyway.

Now, the moment of truth. Do I continue to search for the banana baby food, or do I go around the corner and get Wriley? The pressure mounted, the sweat beads began to form on my temples. I couldn't just pick up any old jar with some flavor that would probably cause Wesley to cry all night! I began to hear the closing notes from Jeopardy. However, I decided, in haste I suppose, because there seemed no time for prayer or counsel, to scrap my search for the bananas, grab the mixed fruits jar—which was pretty close to bananas in my book—and retrieve Wriley. Yes, food for the children is important, but you've got to keep the children around first. It's called priorities, but that's another story.

Decision made, I rounded the corner to catch a glimpse of Wriley sprinting toward the checkout counter, ripping paper from candy as she ran. All of this was, of course, enjoyed by an amused audience of customers and a smiling clerk. When it's not their child, people are amused. Her intent was to get the candy into her mouth before I could say

I rounded the corner to catch a glimpse of Wriley sprinting toward the checkout counter, ripping paper from candy as she ran.

no or ask her to give it to me. She almost succeeded, but I intercepted her hand just short of her open mouth. I then reasoned with her—as best one can reason with a two-year-old—that we must pay for the candy before eating it. Larry Burkett stuff.

I then decided to hold the child firmly—but gently, of course—while I secured the other item I needed. She quickly squirmed out of my arms, and headed for a "hun bun," as she called her favorite breakfast food and one of the five major food groups of two-years-olds. (The others being peppermint sticks, Fruit Loops, french fries, and bubble gum.) She began smashing the pastry with her hands. We've all seen children do this, haven't we? Just mush and squash a fresh, new pastry for no apparent reason. Calling her name no less than five times (something I tend to do when anger erupts), I stopped her from completely destroying the "hun bun" and held her hand (gently, but firmly) as we made our way back to the checkout counter.

Almost home free, I thought, so I released her hand and told her to stand right beside me while I paid. As the clerk was ringing up my bill, I heard the distinctive sound of plastic objects crashing to the ground right behind me. Cringing, I turned, only to discover that my wife's daughter had leveled to the floor what had once been a tall, orderly pyramid of twenty soft drink bottles.

Now I'm not trying to excuse Wriley, but why do stores do this? What real purpose does it serve to stack cola bottles up where the slightest movement can cause bottles to fall all over the place? I've surveyed seventy-three store managers and have not had one answer that made any sense. I encourage you to do your own survey and see if you don't get the same results.

As the clerk handed me my change, I became acutely aware—by virtue of the fact that my leg was experiencing a wet, sticky sensation—that one of the bottles was spewing all over the store. The cola was spraying everywhere. People were jumping around like kangaroos. I also noticed the friendly clerk was no longer smiling. I grabbed the spewing bottle and sheepishly handed it to the clerk as customers continued to scatter out of harm's way. As the clerk made her way to the back with the bottle—mumbling under her breath—I hurried from the store, daughter in tow.

A few days later, certainly not that night, I reflected rationally on that experience and wondered how often it is that I behave in front of God, my Heavenly Father, the way Wriley behaved in front of me that evening. How often do I run for "candy row" and dart off in my own direction when God would have me walk with Him? And when I "escape" from God's will, all too often I find myself knocking over the bottles; it is then that God takes me (gently, but firmly) by the hand and leads me back onto the right path, the path of obedience.

As patient and loving as I am with my daughter as she grows, matures, and yes, bridles her passions, it's a comfort to know that my Heavenly Father is infinitely more patient and loving with me.

Ripped Seams and Baby's Screams

Chris Fabry

Women talk about the agony of childbirth, but the waiting really takes a lot out of the father. We have delivered (and I say "we" because I have been present at each of our seven children's births) at three different hospitals. Three because I am poor at following directions and even poorer at asking for them. Every nerve ending in my body signals panic when it comes time to get there.

Some expectant fathers must learn to contend with expectant mothers who rush to the delivery room at every twitch. I have the opposite trouble. The baby's head could be showing and my wife will say, "Let's wait a few more minutes. We don't want to get there too early."

The Saturday our fifth child was born, my wife awakened me to say, "The kids are watching *Little Mermaid*. I'm going out."

This could only mean one thing. Garage sale. I knew as soon as she said those words that she was going to have the baby that day. Nothing excites and relaxes my wife like a good garage sale, especially one sponsored by an entire subdivision. Big things were ahead.

Thirty minutes later I was standing, holding a bowl of cereal, when Andrea sauntered through the front door. It was damp outside, but her sweatpants seemed a bit more wet than they should be.

"My water broke near Kmart," she said without emotion. She knows it's better to give me a landmark than the actual road name.

"What?!?" I screamed, raisin bran spilling on the counter. Fortunately, it was generic raisin bran and not the expensive stuff. "Why did you come back to the house? You should have called from the hospital!"

"Nonsense," she said, putting down a fifty-pound bag of clothes. "I only stopped once more after it broke. I think I'll take a walk around the neighborhood."

After an hour I convinced her to call the hospital, and when I got on the line they urged me to drag her in. The kids were excited as we drove away, knowing we would soon return with a little brother or sister.

My heart raced. Adrenaline pumped through my driving foot. All my paternal instincts kicked in because I knew this was my only legitimate chance to break the speed limit. But the gas gauge was on red.

"Sorry about that," she said. "I forgot to tell you it needs gas."

I screeched into the filling station, sloshed five dollars' worth of unleaded somewhere near the tank, threw money at the attendant, then careened toward the hospital. Even with the fifth baby I was nervous, mostly because my wife was treating the whole event like she was having a mole removed.

When we arrived the nurses calmed me and handed me some clothes in a bag marked "Large." I took the bag to a tiny bathroom and opened the bag. I was skeptical. I put my feet in and slowly pulled up the pants. The slower I went, the better chance I thought I'd have.

For a moment I forgot baby number five and was whisked back to a particular year of grade school. I'd had a growth spurt (much like the growth spurts I have every year). When picture time rolled around, I tried on the only suit to my name. The sleeves came halfway up my arms, and the buttons were a good four inches away from the button holes. I was in deep trouble.

It was déjà vu with the hospital garb. When the pants finally reached my waist, they were so tight I looked like a shrink-wrapped walrus. I moved like Frankenstein.

I figured the shirt might cover a multitude of groaning seams, so I pulled it as far down as I could. I stepped sideways and opened the bathroom door. My wife looked at me, grabbed her stomach, and said, "I told you not to make me laugh. It hurts too much."

About that time I noticed a funny feeling on my right side. I wedged my shirt up and saw father flesh protruding from the pants. I discovered later I was the first in the history of the hospital to experience a "gown blowout." The nurse came in and covered her mouth with her hand.

"I think you underestimated me," I said.

"I'll get you another one," she replied. Andrea continued

The pants were so tight I looked like a shrink-wrapped walrus.

to giggle and ask that I stay out of sight. In a few minutes the nurse returned.

"Here's a large for you."

"THIS IS A LARGE!" I said, humiliated.

Friends howl when I tell that story and others we've collected. Though the details differ with each birth, the outcome has always been the same: I have felt a sense of unforgettable awe and wonder.

At some point Andrea will look at me with Bambi eyes. (Don't write and tell me Bambi is a boy, I know.) At some point I will desire to pounce on her and do a reverse Heimlich maneuver, but I'll realize I can't. Birthing is a process. You wait nine months; you wait a few hours more.

With Kristen, the doctor came in every few minutes to shake his head and say, "Baby don't wanna come out. Don't understand it."

I wondered how long he went to school to learn that brilliant bit of medicine. I held my tongue. I knew he had more knowledge than me. At least that's what I hoped.

At 10:30 P.M. that Saturday, my wife was squealing and the contractions were frequent. In only twenty minutes she had come further than in the past twelve hours. It was time to start pushing. Suddenly I saw a sight that filled me with wonder. There in the doctor's hands was the head of my fifth child. And then the shoulders, arms, and—whoop—there she is, the whole umbilicaled baby, wet and pink and crying.

"You have a little girl," the doctor muffled through his mask. *What a wonderful man,* I thought. *What a fine, educated, wise medical professional.* The nurse cleaned and warmed Kristen, then put her on the chest of the wide-eyed woman who is my wife.

The thing that made her belly so big only moments before now looked her directly in the eye. Andrea cried and said hello to Kristen Rebecca. I tried to focus the camera but couldn't.

Like life, giving birth is filled with a few spectacular moments and a lot of mundane ones. You drive fast and watch a miracle, but in between there's a lot of standing around. Then it's over and you're left with a life to mold and a two-year fight with the insurance company.

King of the Mountain
Harold B. Smith

I want my boys to look back on our travels together and remember me as one tough Road Warrior; a man whose wits allowed him to make the world—or at least the interstate—his oyster. A man worthy to be admired.

There's probably no better place for a dad to develop his reputation as a first-rate frontier father than the American West.

The American West. Rugged. Desolate. Not for the fainthearted or dull-minded. An environment that only a man's man would dare face. A hostile environment that only a man's man could conquer. Just the place to show Andrew and Kevin my true mettle. It would be minivan against nature.

And so we made our way to the foothills of the Tetons, coursed the Snake River, and explored sections of Yellowstone National Park far off the beaten paths. I served as wise guide and leader, telling my family the history of each region and explaining the forces of nature that gave shape to all we were seeing.

Not that I naturally knew any of this, mind you. It's just that I was usually the one who was handed the informational literature when we entered each attraction. A quick read and, presto, I became the expert!

"Hey, Dad, what causes water to shoot out as a geyser?"

"Good question, Son." With that I'd surreptitiously pull out the appropriate pamphlet, peruse its content, then turn toward my questioning son and deliver an answer that would make even a park ranger envious.

"Son, a geyser is formed due to the pressure created by tectonic shifts beneath the earth's surface, which, in turn, superheat the water."

"Gee, Dad, thanks."

"No problem."

By the time we got to Badlands National Park in South Dakota, I could only imagine how impressed—and proud— Andrew and Kevin were of their frontier father.

If you've ever wondered what the moon was like but didn't have government backing to fly there yourself, then let me suggest a few days in the Badlands. Its crusty, dusty cliffs and pinnacles of dried mud eerily replicate a lunar landscape, as does the park's uniform color of grayish-brown. The only difference, as far as I can see, is the atmosphere, which in the Badlands is more suited to shorts and a tank-top.

We arrived in this other-world near the close of another hot July day. After checking into our motel, we eschewed our usual trek to the information center. *Who needs an informational "crib sheet" here?* I thought. *It's just a lot of dried mud.*

We started our grand adventure at the "Door Trail," so called because of a narrow, winding passageway through two huge mud hills that leads to an endless vista of Badlands mounds. We parked our van in a small, natural amphitheater a few hundred yards in front of the "door." Tall mud mounds surround the amphitheater's circumference, with one smaller mound smack-dab in the center.

Andrew and Kevin flew out of the car and made their way to the nearest mud mountain. Up the side of the amphitheater they fearlessly went, until they reached its summit—about one hundred feet in the air. One false step and it was a fifty-mile drive to the nearest doctor.

Judy tried her best to caution the boys of the very real dangers of a slide down dry mud, but it fell to me, frontier father, to instill awe and wonder in my boys. I climbed the hill in the middle of the amphitheater, and from my muddy pulpit, I bellowed forth.

"Sons, thou shalt wear the appropriate hiking boots before attempting a climb of this magnitude."

"We know, Dad. Mom made us put them on before we came."

"Sons, thou shalt look for pathways made by earlier climbers before forging a new path of your own."

"We know, Dad. We basically took an old path to get up here."

"And sons, thou shalt always test your footing to make sure it is strong and true." I pointed to my own feet, gently rocking my body up and down to emphasize the importance of a firm foundation.

Andrew and Kevin were all ears by now. I felt something akin to a mountain-top experience, standing prophet-like before my worshipful throng of three. Here I was instructing a future generation of Smiths in the ways of taming wild nature. Below me, Judy—looking up at her Road Warrior husband, at the pinnacle of his prowess.

"Be careful, Harold," she said. "I don't want to take three boys to the emergency room!"

I could only laugh at her warning. Perhaps she spoke out of a sense of jealousy. Perhaps she was wishing she were the one straddling the hilltop, that she were the one boldly instructing the flesh of her flesh.

"See, sons. Secure footing. Absolutely essential." I was now jumping up and down, as if to put an exclamation point to this last climbing commandment.

"Yep, boys, absolutely…"

And with that incomplete sentence, the loose dirt under my right foot gave way, transforming my muddy pulpit into a fifty-foot mud-slide.

As I tumbled over the jagged rocks to the amphitheater floor below, I could see Andrew and Kevin running down their hill to come to my rescue (or maybe just to rub it in). I could also see Judy shaking her head in her when-will-he-ever-learn look.

When I finally came to rest on the amphitheater floor, my legs and arms were banged and bruised but happily not broken. Nevertheless, movement was difficult. Nurse Judy tended to the more noticeable cuts and scrapes, and prescribed a strong dose of common sense. The boys, however, were thoroughly impressed.

"Dad, Dad, are you okay?" they asked. "That was a cool fall!"

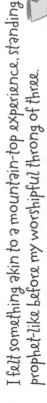

I felt something akin to a mountain-top experience, standing prophet-like before my worshipful throng of three.

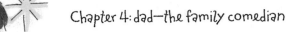

"Now do you see the importance of good footing, sons?" I sternly warned, as if the fall were an object lesson on their behalf. (Dads have to be "quick on their feet" in more ways than one.)

"Yes, we do, Dad," they replied, and then turned and headed for Door Trail. Their dad had looked the Badlands straight in the eye and survived...or had at least been clever enough to save face.

Judy, on the other hand, turned and headed for the car, confident that we'd probably need more Band-Aids and disinfectant before leaving this desolate landscape.

As for me? Well, I just stayed put, nursing my wounds and wondering how I'd overcome my next challenge—getting up off the ground.

The Game of Life

G. Ron Darbee

"Ron, do you have something you'd like to say for yourself?" I asked the question with the entire family assembled. It was several years ago, and Sue was sitting on the couch comforting a distraught Melissa. I was leaning forward in my recliner, and my son Ron stood in the doorway surveying the mood of the room. From all appearances, he was trying hard to remember which of his recent escapades might have led to this unpleasant inquisition. "If you do," I suggested, "this would be a good time to speak up."

"I'm sorry?" Though he chose the correct words, the questioning inflection made me doubt his sincerity.

"Ding-Ding-Ding! Good answer. Good answer!" I applauded like a contestant on a game show we used to watch, then sat quietly, waiting for my son to elaborate on his apology. I was hoping for something resembling a confession of guilt, but soon determined that would be a long time coming.

"Is that it?" he asked, turning toward the kitchen, ready to make a hasty retreat.

"Oh, I don't think so," I answered. "The game's just beginning. Care to explain what you're sorry for?" This is a tactic I employed quite successfully when the kids were younger, often receiving admissions of guilt for transgressions of which I was not yet aware. But over the years they've learned the ins and outs of our parenting techniques, and don't often fall for that approach anymore.

Ron looked around the room again, wisely coming to focus on the image of his sister sniffling and crying on her mother's shoulder. I believe I witnessed the moment of revelation: his eyebrows twitched momentarily, and his jaw clenched shut as his mind pinpointed the probable cause of this most recent summoning. Still, he pleaded the fifth.

"No, but if I did it, I'm sorry."

"Well, Son," I said, "knowing how difficult it is for a creative guy like yourself to keep track of the many events and circumstances life throws your way, I brought along a few visual aids that might serve to trigger your memory. Would you like to see them?"

"I don't think so," Ron said.

"Ehhhhhh," I tried my best to imitate a game show buzzer. "Wrong answer, Son. Let's give it a try, anyway."

Ron shuffled his feet and stared deep into the carpet below, not appearing the least bit enthusiastic about the upcoming presentation of evidence.

"Item number one," I said, pulling a piece of paper from the end table next to my chair and holding it up for display. "This is a birth certificate, and if it pleases the judges"—I looked to my wife and daughter as I continued—"I wish to point out the doctor's signature and the official seal of the state of New York."

Ron glanced up at it momentarily before returning to his inspection of the carpet. I thought I detected the beginnings of a smile on his face, which was confirmation enough—as if I needed it. He appeared to be gnawing on the inside of his cheek, evidently trying to force the grin away.

"Aside from the seal," I continued, "and the high quality paper, the names, the dates, and the official-looking signatures, I have other reasons to believe this document is genuine. Care to know what they are?"

"No?" Again, the boy's inflection was off, and I felt compelled to give him the buzzer.

"Ehhhhhh!"

Melissa, no longer sniffling, appeared to be enjoying herself; Ron, not so much. "I know it's a bit late to explain the rules of our game, Ron, but it is my game. Here are the rules: The pleasant sounding ding signifies a correct answer. The unpleasant buzzer sound, Ehhhhhh," I demonstrated it again for effect, "denotes an incorrect answer. Three incorrect answers—you have already accumulated two—wins you an all-expense paid trip to nowhere for the next two weeks. You'll enjoy no phone calls, no computer time, no Nintendo, and as a specially added bonus, the sponsors have agreed to throw in no allowance. The total value of cash and prizes comes to…let me check my figures…nothing! We call this our Wrath-of-Dad Package."

By this time Ron was trying very hard not to laugh and failing miserably. He knew he was in deep trouble, I knew he was in deep trouble, the neighbors probably had a clue, but we were enjoying ourselves, so why not make discipline fun?

"What do I get if I win?" Ron asked.

"Three incorrect answers wins you an all-expense paid trip to nowhere for the next two weeks."

"You won't, Son; trust me on this."

"Well, if I can't win, I'm not playing."

"Yes, actually you are, Ron. Remember, my rules, my game. But I'll tell you what I'm going to do, since you're one of my favorite contestants. If you answer all of the remaining questions correctly, we'll award you the grand prize, which is a shorter, condensed version of the Wrath-of-Dad Package."

"Is there a consolation prize?" he asked.

"Yes, Ron, but it involves ants and honey and a week in the backyard under a hot sun. I doubt you'd be interested."

"All righty then," Ron said, a phrase he used frequently back then, "let's get this over with."

"OK, back to the game. As I was saying, Ron, we have reason to believe the authenticity of this document—primarily because we were there. In fact, every one of us was there except you. You stayed with your grandparents that day and, if memory serves me, spent the majority of your time messing up your diapers. Your sister served as the principal in the event, which is why her name appears on the birth certificate. I remember your mother quite vividly, as she spent six hours stretched out on a table, screaming in pain, making funny faces, and calling me names. I just tried to stay out of reach and emptied the bedpan when called on. Again, Ron, I'll ask you to trust me on this. I don't forget bedpans."

"That's enough, Dad. I did it." I was getting good at this.

"You did what, Ron?"

"I made a fake adoption certificate on the computer and put Melissa's name on it."

"And then?" He was doing so well, I thought I'd let him run with it.

"If you answer the remaining questions correctly, we'll award you the shorter, condensed version of the Wrath-of-Dad Package."

72

"And then I put it in the box with all the important papers and asked Melissa to show me her Social Security card. I put it right on top, so I knew she would find it."

"Ding-Ding-Ding! Good answer. Good answer! That concludes today's game. The sponsors wish to thank our contestants and the studio audience and invite you all back next time for 'Who Really Blew It This Time?' You can head to your room, Ron. You've got three days in the *hole*" (my term for grounded).

"Three days! But I confessed! Dad, that's not—"

"Four? Did I hear four?"

"Three days, all righty then." Ron rushed off into his bedroom with the speed and grace of a cheetah.

"As for you, young lady," I turned to Melissa, "you need to think things through before you get all upset. At the very least, come talk to Mom or me before you let something like this bother you."

"It looked real," she said.

"Yes, Sweetheart, it looks pretty real," I held up the adoption certificate for her examination, "but if you read the signature here, it says: Ima Knutt. I don't think anyone who works for the state has a name like Ima Knutt. And speaking of the state, how many are there?"

"Fifty," she answered correctly.

"That's right, fifty," I said. "Read what it says on this seal."

"State of Con...Confusion," Melissa read.

"Right, State of Confusion. I don't think that's one of the fifty."

Melissa laughed, Sue laughed, and I laughed; I think I even heard Ron laughing from behind his bedroom door. Sound travels in a house; I keep trying to remember that.

So if your parenting techniques don't measure up to Dr. Spock, don't let it worry you. Mine probably don't measure up to Mr. Spock either. Regardless, I think discipline was meant to make the offender aware of his or her mistakes and provide motivation for improving future behavior. Sometimes—not all the time—we manage to do that without yelling and screaming and swatting a rear end. Nowadays their rear ends are too big to swat anyway, so we're forced to improvise.

Personally, I believe that any reasonable method when applied with consistency usually proves effective. I just hope we don't run out of game shows before our kids leave home.

"Come on, Dad! Not Jeopardy."

"Yes, Jeopardy, Melissa."

"But I don't like that game."

"Too bad. My house, my rules. Now, under the category of 'Words' for five hundred dollars: This four-letter word means to arrive home past the appointed hour. Da dum dum dum—da dum dum, da da dum dum dumm—da dum dum dum dum…" (I really enjoy the sound effects).

"What is 'late'?" Melissa answered.

"Correct," I said. "Remember that tomorrow when you're asked to come home an hour earlier."

"But, Dad!"

"Two hours?"

"OK, an hour. You know, your games really stink, Dad."

"You just have to learn how to play them, Sweetheart."

Chapter 5

merriment for m♥ms

Surprise Pregnancy

Our six-year-old daughter, Annice, was excited that we were planning to have another baby. As her daddy was waving goodbye from the car on the way out of town for a business trip, she shouted to him, "I hope Mommy doesn't get pregnant while you're out of town!"

—FROM "LIFE IN OUR HOUSE," CHRISTIAN PARENTING TODAY (JANUARY/FEBRUARY 1998)

The ABCs of Mommyhood

Nancy Kennedy

Today on *Sesame Street,* we learned about the letters A and L. According to Grover, A is for aardvark, and L is for llama. That may be true for a fuzzy blue Muppet, but it's just not relevant to me and a large, predominantly tired segment of the population— namely, mommies.

No, our world consists of applesauce globs on the wall, and laundry piles everywhere but in the laundry room. So, in the interest of relevancy, the following is a mommy-friendly guide to the alphabet.

A is for active. That's what the church nursery worker calls your child on the day she grabs Thomas P's binkie away from him, spits graham cracker onto the slide, and smacks the Rainey twins on their heads with her stuffed Baby Bop. No mommy wants her child called "active."

B is for breasts, the parts of a new mommy's anatomy that used to belong solely to her, but now are on call 24 hours a day. Sometimes she dreams of a way to separate her breasts from herself and fly to Tahiti. Of course, then there would be nothing to hold up her bathing suit, but that's a chance she's willing to take.

C is for car. Some mommies consider their car to be a second home and have been known to use them for putting on makeup, flossing their teeth and even gargling.

D is for diapers. If mommies aren't changing them, they're smelling them to see if they need changing.

E is for eyes (in the back of Mommy's head). These are standard issue for every mommy and are useful for seeing a 7-year-old stuff contraband Oreos into his shirt while you wash dishes.

F is for forgot. When a mommy asks her 3-year-old, "What did you do with the car keys?" the answer is, "I forgot." When she asks her 5-year-old, "Did you make your bed/brush your teeth/take out the trash?" the answer is, "I forgot."

G is for "goo-goo head," the words that launched World War II. It seems Child A called Child B a goo-goo head, which made Child B take a swing at Child A. Only, when Child A ducked, Child B missed and grazed Child C, who started wailing that Child B was a goo-goo head gorilla and he was going to tell Mommy. That's when Mommy defected from the war and took asylum in the bathroom.

H is for happy, what you expect to be when your oldest child goes off to school. But, as you watch her step on that

E is for eyes (in the back of Mommy's head).

enormous bus, your heart climbs into your throat and doesn't go back until you see her return. That's when you're really happy.

I is for "I don't know." This comes in handy when asked, "Do snakes kiss?" "Where do grasshoppers sleep?" "How many seeds are in a watermelon?" and so on.

J is for "Just a minute!"—what mommies usually yell through the door on the rare occasion they get to use the bathroom, or what they hear whenever they ask a child to pick up his toys/go to bed/wash up for dinner.

K is for kiss. Mommies like kisses. That's how most of them got to be mommies in the first place. Kisses are especially delicious when given by jelly-faced 2-year-olds.

L is for loud, the only volume a toddler has when screaming, "Don't wannt be kwy-it!" while you're trying to get the baby to sleep. It's also the only volume the toddler likes when watching *The Little Mermaid*—11,000 times.

M is for milk. That's what Mommy hates to have leak all over her silk blouse, what babies spit up all over Mommy's silk blouse, and what Mommy cries over when it's spilled at dinner, again all over her silk blouse. Mommy should stop wearing silk blouses.

N is for naps. Ironic thing about naps: The only ones who want them desperately (mommies) are the only ones who can't seem to get them. Instead, naps go to wide-eyed preschoolers who whine, "I'm not ti-errrddd," to which mommies reply, "But I am, so go to sleep!"

O is for "oops." Mommies say it when they splash water on their shirt. Children say it when they accidentally bowl a glass bottle of grape juice through the living room and it hits the (white) wall and breaks and spills all over the (pale gray) carpet. Same word, different connotations.

P is for prayer, something mommies need a lot of. Mommies' prayers are often frantic and specific: "Dear Lord, please let this rash on Laura's stomach not be chicken pox," or, "Heavenly Father, please help Michael to throw up in the bucket and not on the wall."

Q is for quick—what a soapy, naked toddler is as he runs out your front door and in the neighbor's door.

R is for Roto-Rooter. Keep their number handy whenever your resident scientist-in-training dumps a bag of dried lima beans down the kitchen sink and adds a little bit of water and a handful of dirt—the morning the family leaves on a month-long vacation.

S is for scissors, Scotch tape and stationery. Mommies always say they're going to get some and put them away *for Mommy only,* but it never happens. Little fingers find them, use the scissors to cut the siblings' hair, use the entire roll of tape to seal up the magazine you haven't had a chance to read, and soak the stationery in orange juice.

T is for taco night at the drive-thru, because it's 4:30, and the chicken you meant to thaw out is still in the freezer and all that's in the refrigerator is a jar of mustard and a pitcher of Great Bluedini Kool-Aid.

U is for "uh-oh." Uh-oh is similar to oops, but uh-oh is usually followed by, "You're in big trouble," as in, "Uh-oh, Mommy found out."

V is for vacuum, also called "the futility machine." After you have vacuumed the entire house, your 3-year-old will carry an upside-down, open box of Rice Krispies through the living room before you even put the futility machine away.

W is for wiggle, what 2-year-olds do when you want them to stay still. Akin to wiggle is wriggle, what they do to get off your lap and into Daddy's permanent black marker. (See also Quick.)

X is for the big red X your 4-year-old drew on his wall when you thought he was playing with Legos. (X is also for xylem the woody tissue of a plant, which will net 17 points in Scrabble, 51 if you get a triple-word score.)

Y is for "yuck," a handy, all-purpose word that describes everything from the dirt behind your 6-year-old's ears to the baby's strained chicken and peas smeared on the dishwasher door. It's the word you pray your child won't say when Great Aunt Gladys kisses him or when she makes her (yuck) famous breakfast: milk toast and stewed prunes.

Z is for zzzzzz, or lack of zzzzzz's in Mommy's case (see Nap). If all goes according to Mommy's plans, she should get a whole night's sleep in August of 2006. Sweet dreams, Mommy.

Excuse Me?

Marti Attoun

The other day I heard two women in their 60s arguing at the supermarket. I expected one to bop the other with a bag of beans before it was over.

"They probably need a nap," my daughter whispered.

"Oh, they're hyper from scarfing too much junk food," her big brother said. "Or maybe they're hungry. Should I ask them when they ate last?"

OK, OK. So they've heard me make these excuses a few times for their own behavior. But hey, what mother hasn't?…That's always been my own mother's favorite excuse. When my sister, Winnie, flung soggy coffee grounds on the wall and called it art (at age 17), Mom knew Winnie wasn't really at fault. Her diet was the culprit.

"What do you expect? You haven't eaten breakfast in years. I told you it would catch up with you some day."

Excuses drop so naturally from the lips of parents. Right after we rounded the next aisle, my three kids nearly came to blows over the cereal of the week.

"I get dibs on the three-dimensional ghost ring inside."

"Not fair. Last time you got the miniature magic slate with the marshmallow eraser."

"Big deal. You got to sit in the front seat on the ride here."

"And you got out of taking a shower last night because you faked a sore throat. Your throat sounds just fine to me and the rest of these shoppers."

My throat sounded even healthier when I called a truce after a crowd gathered and started placing bets.

"They're just tired," I said to one of the onlookers.

"No, we're not," all three kids answered. "We all skipped showers and went to bed early last night, remember?"

"But you're not eating right," I said sadly.

"We ate boiled fish and broccoli for lunch," they said.

"Well, you're obviously constipated then."

"Nope," all three said.

I remained hopeful. "Is anybody cutting teeth?"

They smiled and showed their full sets.

"Fever? Anybody coming down with a flu bug?" I asked and clapped a hand on their foreheads.

"We feel wonderful," they said. "We just all want the three-dimensional ghost ring."

I thought about drawing straws, but it was easier to grab three boxes of cereal with the flimsy ghost ring inside.

Well, what kind of behavior do you expect from a mom who's overloaded with chocolate and needs a nap?

Is It Real, or Is It Just Mucus?

Charlene Ann Baumbich

Fever, cough (deep cough), hurts, listless, then irritable—very, very irritable. All the symptoms of pneumonia, I told myself at 4:40 A.M.

After five hours of trying to find six inches for me in Brian's twin bed, I was a zombie with a racing heart. Each of his coughs seemed to dig a little deeper, and I kept as still as possible, not even exhaling much of the time, so I could hear him breathing—which I was afraid he was going to stop doing at any moment.

I was damp and tacky myself, but not from fever. That vaporized room at 4 A.M. seemed like a steamy, dangerous jungle. I was miserable, but sleeping with Brian seemed safer and easier than getting out of the warmth of my own bed every five minutes to answer his cries.

I groped for his forehead, touching damp sheets, trying to get a corner of the blanket for myself so I wouldn't be the next one with pneumonia.

I had mentioned to George the night before how I "just knew" Brian was getting really sick.

"How can you tell?" he asked.

"Oh, you know," I said with my most dramatic motherly flair, "a mother can see it in her child's eyes. We *know* these things."

After surviving the night, I thought the morning phone lines for appointments would *never* open. I perched myself right next to the wall phone (actually I was leaning against the wall to keep from falling over) and began speed dialing at 7 A.M. They told me to bring him in at eight.

Waiting in pediatrics is as dangerous as standing in the middle of a six lane highway. Every child has glassy eyes and looks contagious. I tried to shield Brian under my armpit, but then worried I was keeping the fever in, so I simply tried to position him as far away from germs as I could. Right. But I was sure if Brian did have pneumonia, his resistance would be low, and he'd probably succumb to every terrible disease to which he was exposed.

Once we were finally called into the room and they asked Brian to take off his shirt, the waiting *really* began. I hated seeing my shivering baby coughing and moaning and staring into space while I waited. And waited.

A nurse came, took his temperature, and asked several questions about his symptoms. I gave her every detail, including every drip of snot. She never made eye contact with either one of us, but wrote everything down. She closed the door behind her when she left, and we could hear Brian's chart—containing his life-and-death symptoms—shuffling back into the rack on the outside of the door.

An interminable amount of time later, we heard the chart once again scraping against the door. Brian sat up straight and a glimmer of fear crossed his face. Would he need a shot?

Finally the doctor walked in.

"How's Brian today?" the doctor asked while skimming his chart.

Dumb. This doctor is dumb, I told myself. How does he *think* he is? Just look at him!

He asked all the same questions the nurse did. Obviously my evaluation of the doctor was correct; he couldn't even read.

He went through the routine, scoping Brian's eyes and nose, feeling his glands behind his ears, listening to him breathe, then making him cough so he could hear the depths of the rattle.

I sat twisting the strap on my purse, wondering if we'd have to go straight to the hospital and if I had the insurance I.D. card in my wallet.

Finally Dr. Dumb spoke.

"Well, Brian's got a cold."

Hefty clinic bill to find out youngest son has common cold. There should be a Chinese moral in that somewhere.

Believe me, I'm glad it was just a cold. However, I was thinking how much more redeeming it would have been to answer, "I was right, it's zefinolaris, Dear," when George called to check. But to have to say it was just a cold…

I'm incompetent as a mother. No, I'm just behind on sleep. No, I just don't have a medical background. No, I'm paranoid.

No. I was simply wrong, simply human. And I'm sure I'd take

the same precautions the next time. My children are too precious to risk.

Well, maybe the sun will shine tomorrow and dry up Brian's runny nose so I can make that long postponed trip to the grocery store. I've already served the it-must-be-time-to-grocery-shop casserole. Everyone recognizes it by its brownish color which comes from mixing whatever was in the vegetable bin, sprouts and all.

In the meantime, Sniffles and I will watch the raindrops trickle and mingle as they run down the window. And I'll console my tired body and fragile ego with that old saying, "It's better to be safe than sorry." I imagine a mother invented that one.

Get on Board That Potty Train

Nancy Kennedy

I know from experience: the one thing mothers care about most passionately is potty training. The problem is, we're just not content to let things happen naturally. It's as if our children's skill in keeping their Lion King panties dry is a direct indicator of our worth as parents. Not only that, it becomes a contest among mothers. ("All of my babies were trained by their first birthday." "Oh, so late? Mine were all trained by nine months.")

I well remember my first guinea pig—I mean, daughter. I remember setting up Alison's potty chair in the living room, sitting her on it, and keeping her on it until she did something. *Anything.* I tried everything: "I'm a Big Girl" charts with stickers, big girl underwear. (She called it, "big geeeerl undaweeer.") I even bribed her with M & Ms and wild applause for every tinkle.

I received my own toilet training in the hardware department at Sears. As the story goes, I was a child of even temperament who just happened to have her own timetable (or else I was a rebellious, headstrong little tyke; it all depends on who tells the story). Mom would place me on the toilet at regular intervals (not my regular intervals, mind you) and ask me to do what I preferred doing in my diaper.

The Sears incident took place when I was about three. Still in diapers, I went with my dad to do whatever dads go to do in the hardware department at Sears. And in the middle of us doing it, I had to go. Right then. Right there.

I tugged and I pulled and I yanked my diaper free. Then I pulled my dress up around my waist, marched over to the display toilets, and hopped on the nearest one. The story has a happy ending. I'm not warped or emotionally disturbed, and at age forty I can use the potty all by myself (and have been doing so for a few years now). But to this day, I have an irrational fear of the bathroom displays at Sears.

Recently I met a woman in Kmart. In her shopping basket was a toy golf club set, a potty chair, and a toddler named Jacob. Although I didn't ask, the woman began talking about IT. "He'll go in the yard. He'll go at the park. He'll go against the car tires. He hits the knot hole on the tree out back, and once he hit—with perfect aim—the entire length of the back fence." She took a breath and continued, "He goes everywhere. He goes around the toilet, but *he won't go in it.* I've tried making a game out of it: 'Aim for the Cheerios in the water, Jacob!' I've tried *everything.*"

Hearing us talk, a third woman stopped. Her shopping cart was filled with packages of training pants, a potty chair, and a toddler named Erin. "Just last week," she offered, "we were in the ladies' room at a very crowded restaurant. As we walked back to our table, Erin announced, 'Give Mommy a sticker—she went potty all by herself!'"

In a short time, the aisle filled with mothers, toddlers, potty chairs, and potty paraphernalia. As we stood there, passionately discussing the bathroom habits of little ones, the very subjects of our discussion—as if on cue—covered their ears with their hands while ringleader Jacob shouted, "NO MORE POTTY TALK!"

But potty talk is what moms do. How to do it, when to do it. Potty chair or regular toilet? Training pants, big girl underwear, Pull-Up disposables? Do we call it pee-pee or urine? Poo-poo or…what? Do we employ what one parenting magazine called the "Sit-'Em-On-the-Pot Plot" or let the child decide in her own time? What if she's not trained by preschool? What if she's not trained by kindergarten? Will I still be changing her diapers the day of her high school graduation?

When Laura, my second daughter, came along, I opted for the *qué será, será* approach. By then I was in my thirties and tired. I'd never heard of a high school graduate in diapers, so I figured she'd either get the hang of it or be in *The Guinness Book of World Records* as the oldest living diaper wearer.

By age two-and-a-half she had reached a point where she could get her own diaper, lay it out on the floor, take off her wet one, climb on the dry one, and pull it up across her bottom.

That's when I decided if you're big enough to change your own diaper, you're probably big enough to use the potty.

Out went *qué será, será*. In came Intensive Potty Training 101. "Laura, you want to wear big girl underwear like Alison, don't you?"

That's when I decided if you're big enough to change your own diaper, you're probably big enough to use the potty.

"No."

"Laura, you want to go in the potty for Mommy, don't you?"

"No."

"Laura, you want to go for Daddy, don't you?"

"No."

I changed tactics. "Laura, if you go in the potty, you can flush it bye-bye."

"Don't want to."

I changed tactics again. "Sit on the pot and GO!"

She didn't. She wouldn't. Instead of happy sounds of tinkle echoing through the house, there was weeping and wailing and gnashing of teeth—mine. Meanwhile, Laura happily changed her own diaper and calmly played with her Legos in her room.

After a week or so of unsuccessful training, I reached my limit. In a last-ditch desperate measure, I grabbed my car keys, tucked Laura in her car seat, gave her a boxed apple juice to drink, and went off…to the hardware department at Sears. I figured: *It worked with me. Maybe it'll work with my offspring.*

It didn't.

Laura looked over the display toilets, said she liked the blue one, then asked if we could throw pennies in the mall fountain. No bursts of inspiration. No sudden urges to hop on the pot. *Guinness Book of World Records, here we come,* I thought.

Then one day Laura decided diapers were for babies and she was a big girl. That was that. Hallelujah, Amen.

All along, I had missed God's perfect answer to the problem: "There is a time for everything, and a season for every activity under heaven" (Ecclesiastes 3:1).

Even potty training.

Chapter 6

good sports—
laughter on the playing field

Big-Inning Baseball

It is an old baseball joke that big-inning baseball is affirmed in the Bible, in Genesis. "In the big inning, God created...."

—FROM MEN AT WORK: THE CRAFT OF BASEBALL, GEORGE F. WILL

Has Anyone Seen My Husband's Camouflage?

Chonda Pierce

There are some great big differences between men and women.

After all these years of marriage, my husband is finally starting to buy his own clothes, only everything is green and brown. He says these are the perfect colors when he goes out to the country. Nothing can see him.

I don't understand this. I buy clothes specifically so that someone *will* see me!

"Who is it you don't want to see you?" I asked.

"Not who," he said, "*what*."

"*What* is it you don't want to see you?"

"The live game. You know—deer, turkey."

"Opossums?"

"Naw, I don't care if they see me."

"Then don't dress like the front of a Ford."

"Huh?"

"Just joking."

Sometimes he wants me to go with him to see the gorgeous "game." One day I said I would go. I'm not sure why. I put on my new Kathy Lee Gifford sweater from Wal-Mart—fuchsia with a bit of turquoise around the neck and just a hint of olive woven through. I put on some cute little diamond earrings, the kind they sell on the Home Shopping Network for $2 each, if you buy fifty pair. I was all set to go when my husband entered the room. (He had dressed in the garage.) He looked like a tree—green, brown, drab olive, and fungus-colored.

He took one look at me and said, "You're not wearing *that* are you?"

"What's wrong with this?" I tugged at the sweater and turned around so he could see the back of it as well before he rushed to judgment. "Can't you see the olive?"

"Well, for one, you'll scare off the game."

"What game?"

"The game I hope to see."

"But I thought deer were color blind."

He was looking right at me, but for a moment his mind zipped off far, far away. The wheels inside his head were turning, the way they do whenever I lay down a cold, hard fact that somehow stuck in my head but had gotten past him. I knew what he was doing. He was rewinding every episode of *Wild Kingdom* and *Hunting with Howard and Jim* that he had ever watched on the Sports Channel to find that piece of information. He blinked several times, and that's how I knew he was back.

"But I thought deer were color blind."

"Where did you hear that?" he asked. His lips were dry, his breathing ragged.

I shrugged. The wrong answer here could throw him into a state of shock. I recognized the need to withdraw. The wrong answer at this point—something like The Discovery Channel or ESPN II—could have devastating effects. I would have to be careful. So I said, "Oprah."

For the longest moment he stood still. Then a wave of relief washed over his face like rain. He even chuckled. "For a minute there I thought you were serious. Come on, you look good in earth tones. Go ahead and change. I'll be waiting in the Jeep."

My husband doesn't stalk animals to hunt them; he just likes to stalk them for the sake of stalking them. (Wasn't a law passed recently against that? Somebody help me.) Soon we were thick into a jungle of briars and low-hanging limbs. (I was so glad he had talked me out of my fuchsia sweater.) Every so often he would turn to me and point at the ground, where I would see a couple of half-moon tracks grouped close together that were supposed to be hoof prints.

A vision of Elmer Fudd flashed into my mind—not that my husband looks like Elmer Fudd, but remember the episode in which he was hunting for "wabbit," and he looked straight into the camera (what an actor!), and said, "You must be bewrry, bewrry qwiet"?

My husband would point to the track and mouth the words, big and slowly, "Look, deer!"

I would mouth back, "Oh," and nod that I understood, just in case my lips were too hard to read. We did this for five miles.

Point. "Look, deer!"

"Oh," Nod.

Point. "Look, deer!"

"Oh," Nod.

When we finally circled back to the Jeep, I told him how disappointed I was that we hadn't actually seen any deer, just their tracks, but that I was sure some lovely game lived in those woods.

He rubbed his chin thoughtfully and scanned the thicket we had just come from. "Yeah. They can hide pretty good sometimes. I'm not sure what happened. Maybe..." he paused, as if considering whether to even mention this tiny maybe, "...maybe it was the earrings." He shrugged and opened the Jeep door for me—the bright red, look-at-me-driving-through-the-woods Jeep.

I put a hand to my earlobe and felt the shape of a big, fake, Home Shopping diamond. I started to tell him about a particular episode on a video I'd seen—I think it was a Gary Smalley video. It was about a man who couldn't appreciate that his wife tried to dress herself up for him from time to time, and if that man couldn't hold his woman every now and then and tell her how beautiful she was, then somebody needed to wake up or—but David already was cranking up the monster engine, scaring all the deer deeper into the forest.

Later that night I discovered something about my husband's wardrobe. It is invisible—especially on the floor. I led him through the living room, up the steps, and into the bedroom, every so often stopping to point. I'd mouth the words, so he could read my lips. "Look, dear." I pointed to his green-and-brown shirt.

"Oh," he answered with a big nod and then reached down to scoop it up.

"Look, dear," I said, pointing to the green-and-brown socks.

"Oh," and he nodded.

I thought about wearing some camouflage pajamas to bed some night with my handsome Elmer Fudd. If I do, I believe either one of two things will happen: He won't even see me, or—didn't you see that *Oprah* episode?

Did I mention that there are some big differences between men and women?

Hanging Up the High Tops
Jim Killam

In an event drenched with symbolism, my friend and I recently put together an adjustable basketball hoop in my driveway. Afterward, we were too exhausted to do anything but watch the kids shoot baskets.

At age 35, I am announcing my retirement from competitive sports. This is not about money, nor is it about pride (my athletic ability has produced neither). It's about finally exorcising the basic male need to be seen as a jock.

It's also about pain. I personally am opposed to pain, especially the kind caused by doing something that used to require no effort—like jogging the length of a gymnasium.

The applause you heard during the preceding announcement came from my wife. She's been worrying that I'd somehow be killed playing church-league basketball. Her fears might have been based on me coming home after games looking like I'd been dragged behind a tractor for two hours. This was the result of a training regimen that involved showing up for a game having experienced nothing remotely resembling exercise in the past week. So by the second quarter, I'd have been happy to be dragged around by a tractor because at least I wouldn't have had to move under my own power.

I suppose, sooner or later, all would-be athletes come to the realization that we're embarrassing ourselves in front of strangers and we really just need to go home and take up needlepoint. Still it's as difficult for the male ego to accept as it is for our wives to understand. I'm the same age as Michael Jordan, who even in retirement can whip anyone on the planet in one-on-one.

The great ones accept aging gracefully, bowing out before they are embarrassed by younger, faster, stronger players. (Of course, already having earned a bazillion dollars makes this decision a lot easier.) The clods, on the other hand, wait for a subtle sign that maybe it's time to pack it in. In my case, the sign was that my bones started breaking when I played basketball. During a low-speed game at a church picnic, I pivoted wrong, tumbled to the concrete and snapped my ankle—all without being so much as breathed on by another player.

"Maybe someone is telling you that you should give this up," my wife said in that I-told-you-so tone on the way to the doctor's office. With my ankle the size of a softball, I knew she was right. But I wasn't happy about admitting the ultimate defeat: failing to achieve sports greatness at any level.

Despite my 6' 5" height and reasonable amount of coordination, I never was what you'd call a star athlete. In fact, I warmed the bench for an incredibly mediocre high school basketball team. I suspect I made the team because I could dunk, which fired up the other players during warm-ups. One problem was that I weighed 170 pounds and could be pushed around by opposing cheerleaders.

The other was a certain, shall we say, flair for embarrassment. One time the coach put me into an overtime game to control an important tip-off. As I turned my head to decide where to tip the ball, the referee tossed it up (the ball, not my head). My feet never left the floor, and we ended up losing the game. Thereafter my high school nickname was Tip.

Later I turned to college intramurals and church leagues, hoping to gain that competitive edge that would lead to respectability. I wasn't bad for a few years, despite numerous ankle injuries. These required me to tape my ankles before playing, which in turn required me to shave my legs from mid-calf down. That's fine for basketball, but try going to the beach and seeing every mother pull her small children close as you walk by, the sun glaring off your pasty shins. Church-league glory had its price.

Then my wife and I had kids. Slowly, my athletic energy dwindled and my skills diminished. I still can beat my sons, ages 10 and 12, in driveway hoops. But I can't dunk anymore. And in the next few years, the boys will develop jump shots as I develop male-pattern baldness.

That's okay, handing the torch to your own kids. But it's time to stop being humiliated by guys who were still in diapers the first time I dunked a basketball. Guys with lots of free time who hang out at the gym practicing no-look passes while I am home grading papers, fixing toilets and picking Fruity Pebbles out of the family-room carpet. Not that I'm bitter.

I held on as long as I could. In fact, two equally 30-something friends and I entered several three-on-three tournaments in the past few years and were consistently humiliated by guys who actually had practiced together, the show-offs. Our record upon retirement remains unblemished by victory.

There was something nice, though, about having our wives come to cheer for their warriors. At game's end, they'd always be there to offer words of encouragement: "See, I told you it was time to give this up."

So that's it for me. No more competitive basketball, even though there's an ad in today's paper for a three-on-three tournament next month. Hey wait a minute! They have a 35-and-over division.

Nah. I kinda like having hair on my ankles again.

Can't Beat Fun at the ld Ballpark
(Although Our Boys Have Tried)
Lynn Bowen Walker

My husband, Mark, and I are what you might call diehard San Francisco Giants fans. We are determined that our progeny will rejoice in a well-executed hit and run. No matter that after the first two pitches of the game, the children are ready to go bye-bye. My husband and I are as excited as rookie pitchers: "This is baseball! You kids are gonna love it!"

We schlepped our kids to the ballpark when they were babies; we schlepped them when they were toddlers; we are schlepping them now as little boys.

This might not sound impressive until you realize just what it entails. Our first post-baby year, starry-eyed in love with our bundle, we set off to the ballpark. Our shoulders sagged from hauling infant equipment, but we were filled with optimism. We sat in our seats, baby Ben nestled in frontal pouch. We had a hot dog in one hand, a soda in the other. A green field, a sunny day. Life couldn't get any better.

Then came the peeps. Then cries. Then shrieking demands to be walked. Mark graciously offered to circle the stadium till the baby settled down. That was in the first inning. I did not see them again until the ninth.

Clearly, this was not going to be easy.

But we weren't giving up. The following year, new baby Jake occupied the front pack. Visor-shaded Ben was relegated to the stroller. It is, we found, an interesting challenge to get a stroller up the escalator when you have a kangaroo cleaving to your front and two diaper bags bigger than the umpire's belly swinging from both shoulders.

Between trips to the bathroom to change odoriferous pants, and trips to the concession stand to divert our son from using pompoms as "wigs" on the lady in front of us, we didn't see a whole lot of the game. But we figured just getting to the ballpark, finding our seats, and eventually making it home without veering off the freeway (*you* try steering with one hand and waving a bottle at the back seat with the other, hoping desperately to hit your two-inch round target) was an accomplishment at least as great as, say, erecting the pyramids.

One would think by now we had suffered enough baseball with our kids. One would be wrong. It was the next year that we hit upon the Family Baseball Vacation.

The place was Houston. The time: spring. It was the first homestand of the Astros, in their 25th year playing in the Astrodome—a place the media-relations people modestly termed "The Eighth Wonder of the World." There was only one hitch: It was a night game. With a toddler and a preschooler.

Still, we were determined to enjoy ourselves. We walked Ben and Jake down stairs and up ramps, ignoring their pleas for an inflatable bat. Once in our seats, the children were unimpressed by the "Eighth Wonder of the World." So what if an 18-story building could fit inside the Astrodome? So what if the building contained more than 4,500 painted skylights? The boys were more intrigued with jumping on the folding seats, soon, of course, cracking heads with the toddlers in the next row, who were jumping on their daddy's toes. They delighted at seeing my husband's feet ride the brown sticky river of spilled soda. They joined in the chimes of neighboring children, "It's over, it's over, it's over." The second half of the first inning had not even begun.

Ah, you can't beat fun at the old ballpark.

Why do we do this to ourselves? Because, for one thing, baseball is a big part of both Mark's and my histories. And, pitiful as it may sound, it is also one of the few hobbies Mark and I share. We have tried to come up with other common interests, but our failure has been dismal.

But perhaps the most compelling reason we are reluctant to abandon baseball lies in the nature of parenthood itself. In becoming parents, we'd already had to give up sleeping in and sex. It hardly seemed fair we'd have to give up baseball, too. Besides, what other public entertainment place can you think of where your son can wear his backpack on his head, scrunch up his nose and pretend to be a "wolf-er-ine" and no one even notices? (It's because all the other fans are busy untangling their own wolf-er-ines.) Where else can much-loved Baby Bunny accompany us, thrust heavenward in Jakie's arms during the seventh inning stretch?

I do have one final confession to make, however. Last year, cereal eaters who saved enough box tops could earn free passes to the Major League baseball game of their choice. For weeks I quietly, methodically hoarded boxtops. When I had all I needed I secretly mailed them in, and met the mailman out at the box before the children could even see what had arrived.

The envelop finally came. The boys never found out.

It was free Giants tickets.

For two.

It's All Downhill from Here

Ken Davis

Skiing didn't come easily; I didn't even know skiing language. My first day on the hill I heard someone yell, "Ski, ski!" He was alerting me that a ski was careening down the hill—by itself.

When I first learned to ski, safety straps weren't yet in use. If you lost a ski, it kept racing down the hill at a speed approaching that of a bullet. I've seen a picture of a ski that penetrated a car door. When you hear someone yell, "Ski!" you're supposed to turn and look uphill so you can see what it's going to penetrate.

I didn't know this language. I thought someone was mocking my blundering attempts to make it down the hill. "Ski, ski!" they yelled.

"I am, I am!" I yelled back.

Later that day, I skied to the top of the hill and came down screaming "Toboggan!" People simply skied into the woods to get out of the way. Imagine what *that* would look like embedded in the side of a car door.

Lesson One: If you're going someplace strange, learn the language.

I decided I needed to take a lesson. I was very intimidated by the instructor. "My name is Jacques Benoit [pronounced *Shock Benwah*]," he said in his suave French accent. "Today," he continued, "I ham goeeeng to teesh you how to fall down."

"Excuse me, Mr. Benwah," I interrupted. "I just paid you twenty-five dollars—I'd appreciate it if you would teesh me how to stand up."

I asked for my money back and abandoned the lesson. Dozens of adoring students stayed and learned how to fall gracefully to the ground on command. Later that same day, their skis would cross and they'd all be doing the same clumsy face-plant I was doing. But my fall would seem more graceful, because I was twenty-five dollars richer.

Lesson Two: Never pay money to learn how to fail.

After quitting the lesson I stood in line at the lift with the more experienced skiers. I think I needed more training—I fell while standing in line. My fall triggered a domino reaction. By the time it stopped, there were thirty unhappy people lying on the ground. I didn't want them to know I'd caused the crash, so I just lay there yelling, "Who fell?"

I finally got on the chair lift. Within seconds I was hundreds of feet in the air. I was terrified! I looked over and saw for the first time a man sitting next to me. I have no idea where he came from. Between us was a steel post that connected to the lift cable. It was the only solid thing within reach. I wrapped my entire body around the post. "God loves you and has a wonderful plan for your life," I informed the stranger. "But this is my post. If you touch this post, you will meet Jesus today."

Lesson Three: Take every opportunity to be a blessing.

As I got off the lift, I fell again. I don't know why, but they always ice down the little hill where you get off the lift. I slid to the bottom and desperately tried to stand up. I'd just about made it to my feet when the next person off the lift crashed into me and we both went down.

They don't stop the lift—not for anything. I lay there in the traffic pattern as body after body joined the wiggling pile.

"Who fell?" I screamed as I extracted myself from the group.

Within minutes I was in trouble again. I was standing at the lip of a "black diamond" ski slope—terrified. This slope looked as if it plummeted straight down all the way to a place that does not freeze over. Some of Shock Benwah's practical wisdom came to mind. "If you ever come to a hill that is too difficult for you," he'd said, "then you must traverse!"

Traverse is a French word meaning, "Go across ze hill until you come to ze trees." This allows you to progress more slowly than pointing the skis straight down the hill. "When you get to the othair side of zee slope," Shock instructed, "zen go into a snowplow turn and traverse ze ozzer way."

On this hill, halfway through my first snowplow turn, I was doing eighty miles per hour. I decided there would be no more snowplow turns. I invented my own turn called, "Sit down/turn around." It required twisting my body into positions from which I might never recover. But at least I wasn't moving.

Lesson Four: When in doubt, sit down for a while.

Four hours later I was only fifty feet down the "black diamond" hill. I wouldn't have made it that far if I hadn't been wearing slippery clothes. As I lay there with sweat dripping from every pore in my body, I heard a noise. I looked uphill just in time to see a young boy about twelve years old, swooping down the hill in perfect skiing form. His hair streamed behind him and his cheeks were red from the wind. "Go for it!" he yelled as his body streaked toward me with athletic grace.

I stuck him with my pole. "Go for that, you little shish kebab!"

Lesson Five: If you're old, don't watch young people ski.

But do ski. I've spent years laughing with hundreds of thousands of people over my experiences on the slope. I've met hundreds of those people who identified with the struggles I faced. They've laughed and spoken with animation as they remembered their adventures. The most energetic and exciting people I know are people who keep exploring the boundaries of life—pushing the envelope.

Adventure is not just for on-the-edge thrill-seekers. And the Creator of this beautiful world never meant to reserve its enjoyment for the "experts."

Athletically challenged people like me should ski.

The tone-deaf should sing.

God didn't create couch potatoes.

Chapter 7

viva la difference—

hum♥R between men and women

High Hopes

Men marry women hoping they won't change; women marry men hoping they will.

—FROM MORE HOLY HUMOR, CAL AND ROSE SAMRA

Hurry Up, We're Going to Be Late

Joey O'Connor

I was flying down the freeway.

No, Jimmy, I wasn't a happy camper.

My wife was not making me happy. You had to be there.

Like a raving, Gumby-eyed lunatic at the controls of an intercontinental Concorde jet ready to snap the exploding whip of the sound barrier, I VAAROOOOM-DAHed down the cow pasture-lined highway at over one hundred miles an hour. On the wrong side of the road. With the pink rental car speedometer tickling 107, nothing was moving faster than this Hertz hurricane of fury except my eyes, looking everywhere at once for Barney Fife to pull me over.

Clutching a pathetic, wrinkled rental car map, I precariously balanced the steering wheel in my left hand while attempting to read the microscopic words and squiggles directing me to the car rental return area. Blood surged through my veins as my anger spiked at the thought of a British map-maker laughing at silly, frantic Americans careening into smelly cow fields while trying to read the extra-fine print.

"Uuuggghhh," I screamed as I locked my leg onto the accelerator and launched a series of stammered outbursts audible only to the empty passenger seats. "WE'RE GO-ING-TO-MIIISSSS-THEEE-PLA-AA-A-NE!"

Maybe I was temporarily going insane? Maybe I ate some bad British burger and had contracted the "Mad Cow" disease?

No way. This wasn't my fault.

My wife, Krista, and mother-in-law, Betty, were at the Heathrow International Airport terminal where I had dropped them off fifteen minutes earlier.

It was the end of our London vacation and I was doing my best Clark Griswold impersonation.

An hour earlier, I was told we were going to spend "just a few minutes" at the Laura Ashley shop in downtown London. Just real quick.

"You wait in the car," they told me.

Laura Ashley-Smashley-Mashley.

I waited. That was my first mistake.

"Just a few minutes" turned into an hour as Krista and Betty oohhed and aahed over floral prints, elegant sweeping dresses, mommy and me matching outfits, bedspreads, wallpaper, curtains, stationery sets, toilet roll holders, Prince Charles earwax removal kits…you get the picture.

Three times I sounded the five-minute warning.

Should've called James Bond.

A handsome 007 would have stolen their attention.

Should've called Henry VIII.

Didn't Anne Boleyn shop at Laura Ashley?

Now I was a lost Mario Andretti wannabe fumbling over fouled-up directions, doing God only knows how many kilometers per hour, while coaching myself in the fundamental driving techniques of the Motherland, "Stay to the *left* of the road. STAY LEFT. STAY LEFT."

The plane was leaving, not boarding, for America in fifteen minutes.

Bingo. Finally found the car return. Stormed inside and was warmly greeted by a cordial British car rental return manager who queried, "Might you be Mr. O'Connor? I just received a phone call from your wife who's wondering where you are."

Visualize rage.

After silently simmering on a shuttle bus slower than a late-afternoon English tea, I bounded off the bus and through the electronic doors at the main terminal. Standing next to an x-ray security station, Krista and Betty waved me down and yelled their only foreign words of the whole trip, "Hurry! We're going to miss the plane! What took you so long?"

Excuse me? Did I just hear what I just heard? What took ME so long?

Mother, daughter, and the fang-bearing American Werewolf in London son-in-law dashed through the first security station where polite British officers scanned our Laura Ashley bags and checked for terrorist bombs. I wouldn't be a bit surprised if one of Laura's clerks slipped a big boomer in

The plane was leaving, not boarding, for America in fifteen minutes.

the bag. Good ol' Laura certainly terrorized me all afternoon long. A few more scenarios like this and I'd be ready to get back to my Irish roots by joining the IRA.

We sprinted twenty paces only to be halted again by a second security station.

"Why are there so many x-ray machines?' Krista said out loud. "We're never going to make the plane!"

The snapping, popping, stinging spark of my anger finally detonated.

"Krista! This! Is! Not!! The! United! States! Of! America! We-are-in-a-foreign-country-where-bombs-explode-eh-ver-ree-hee-day!"

When the smoke finally cleared, my claws retracted and the three of us began running toward our gate through a marathon series of hallways. Our gate, #1,851, was the last gate, the farthest away from the curb, about as close as you can get to the border of the former Soviet Union.

Dressed in wool sweaters, thick overcoats, and long every-thing for the nip of English weather…plus, loaded down with—yes, you got it—Laura Ashley dresses, Laura Ashley kids' clothes, Laura Ashley power tools, sweat poured down our faces as we half-ran, half-speed-walked down the labyrinthine hallways of Heathrow International Airport.

In my mind, anger bubbled and popped in a thick meaty stew. *Fine. This is just fine…I hope we miss the stupid flight. I don't care one bit. I hope, I hope, I hope we miss the plane.*

Bumbling along, I looked at the sweat-drenched faces of Krista and Betty. They both looked back at me and went ballistic in sidesplitting laughter.

Reciting the polar opposite of what I was thinking, they launched another volley of laughter and screamed, "We can make it! C'mon...keep going! We can make it!"

Tears streamed down Krista's and Betty's faces as they cried all the louder at the sight of the tortured scowl on my mug. Open mockery.

Funny. Real funny. Laughter as a defense mechanism, right?

Finally, we arrived at our gate and were met by an airline attendant wildly waving her arms.

"Hurry, they're going to shut the airplane door," she cried.

Huffing, puffing, perspiring, almost expiring, we boarded the airplane. A flight attendant stopped us in the aisle and apologized, "I'm sorry, but your seats in Coach Class were taken. We had to bump all of you to First Class."

Krista's eyes lit up like landing lights and met my bloodshot, narrowed slits. Tilting her head to one side, she beamed in surprise. "See, isn't it a good thing we were late!"

The Upchuck That Saved Our Marriage

Charlene Ann Baumbich

A miracle has taken place on Second Street, where George and I live. In fact, it is parked in our driveway. Perhaps the new car itself isn't the miracle; but rather, the fact that George and I are still together.

You would think that by now we would have learned how to accommodate each other's polarized philosophies concerning major purchases. But instead, we have learned to gear up for the battle that will swallow us alive until the sales receipt is in our hands, thus disgorging us from the belly of the whale.

You see, George is a firm believer of easing into things, especially new cars. His shopping cycle goes something like this: read, explore, talk, compare, drive. Repeat. Notice the word *buy* is not in this cycle.

I, on the other hand, say "Let's go buy a car—today."

And so, as the time to make a major purchase draws near, we

begin by talking sweetly to each other, hoping that kind words and attitudes will ward off any similarities to past experiences. Which, of course, they do not.

Nevertheless, we cheerfully begin Phase One by independently browsing. George eyeballs a couple of makes on his way home from work; I venture behind-the-wheel a few times in showrooms during my daily outings. George picks up a couple of brochures; I form a few aesthetic opinions. We discuss our findings over dinner.

Already we don't agree. But in our unending quest to maintain peace, we cheerfully decide to give the other guy's favorite another look. Yuck.

This moves us directly to Phase Two: an exhausting search for possibilities. Evenings are spent prowling through lots, crawling in and out of cars that salesmen insist are just what we're looking for. Price tags continue to astound us. We play with the notion of keeping our old vehicle—until it coughs and sputters its death rattle, reminding us why we began this venture.

Finally, we enter Phase Three: I fall in love with a new model. It fits me like a glove. It has power everything. It has a moon roof, which is even better than a sun roof. It has a cool console with the gear do-jobby on the floor. It has leather seats and a four-speaker stereo system. Although I may be sitting perfectly still on the showroom floor, my mind is speeding us down the highway on a romantic weekend getaway.

Then I look at George and am slam-dunked into Phase Four: He doesn't fit in any car that fits me like a glove. He points to the top of his head, drawing my attention to the static electricity that has sucked his hair up to the bottom side of the moon roof. He thumps the side of his foot against the console to emphasize that consoles take up valuable space he needs for his size thirteen shoes. He thinks talk radio programs are as good as audio bliss gets, so why do we need all those speakers? He says the engine is too small and babbles something about gear-ratio something or other. Our faces start to lose their patient grins.

Off to another dealer where Phase Five commences: George finds his dream car. It has loads of space and not a lot of extras. It has digital nothing. It's the worst color ever conceived by a human. Its ratios or whatever are all in order. It is the quintessential Old Geezer's car.

Which leads us to Phase Six: *What am I doing married to this person?* And our relentless pursuit continues.

Eventually, Phase Seven finds a place in our lives: a car we can both live with and perhaps even enjoy. It is a short-lived moment of bliss, however, because as we enter the salesperson's office Phase Eight opens its jaws: the Sticker Price.

Thus begins the true test of our "for-better-or-worse" vows. We hold our breath, hoping the test-driver is actually able to return in our trade-in. Finally the driver reappears in the cubicle and shakes his head as he hands the keys to our salesman. It's downhill from there.

He names a price. We laugh. He asks us what we had in mind. We tell him and he laughs. Runs are made to and from a hidden manager. George and I squabble about what we each believe is a fair price to pay. I want this over so the rest of our lives can resume; George isn't making a deal until every deliberate step is taken during this car-buying dance.

Many people actually end up buying a car at this point. We don't. After five hours, *five hours,* we leave to find a "bet-

George isn't making a deal until every deliberate step is taken during this car-buying dance.

ter deal." Phase Nine gulps us down: hostility. With car dealers, with one another. Why do we have to play this game?

About the time I announce I just can't take it anymore, George remembers yet another dealer we haven't tried. He'll check it out tomorrow on his way home, he says.

They have what we're looking for. We meet with the salesman that very evening and repeat our let's-try-to-buy-a-car scenario. After much bantering, this guy's best-deal price turns out to be higher than the last one. We drive home in our rattletrap, which suddenly feels conspicuously like a digestive tract.

George remembers still another place we haven't been. We decide we will browse the lot the next day, which is Sunday, when they're not open.

Eureka! "Car No. 2299" it says in bold black letters on a sticker in the window. I spring a new plan on George.

"How about this? Let's decide what we're willing to pay. You go to work tomorrow and I'll come here first thing in the morning with the checkbook. I'll hand them the keys to our car for a test drive while I tell them which car we want to buy. I'll offer to write the check if the price is right. I promise, George, I won't pay a penny more than we agree. What do you say?"

"Promise? You won't pay a penny more?"

"Promise."

"Deal."

At the crack of 9 A.M. I hand the salesman my keys and explain my plan. As he gives my keys to the test driver, he takes down some pertinent information. My heart thumps. The salesman gives me a price that's worse than the last one. I explain I'm disappointed. He asks me what price I had in mind. I tell him. He says, "If I can get you that price, you'll write the check?"

"Yes," I tell him.

He disappears and returns with the head honcho, whose fingers begin to tap dance on the calculator. He writes down a few things, then quotes me a price that is $91.28 higher than George's and my price.

"This is the best I can do," he says. "I can't even get rid of that twenty-eight cents."

I feel like I'm in a meat grinder. "Is my marriage worth $91.28?" I silently ask myself.

I ask God to give me strength. I remember saying, "Promise" to George.

What if I left and we didn't buy this car? Could our marriage take one more day of this? Absolutely not! How long could George stay mad? I grab a piece of scrap paper lying on the desk and act like I'm tallying up numbers to give myself time to think. Finally, but not easily, my conscience wins.

I put the checkbook in my purse and say, "I'm sorry you can't do anything about the twenty-eight cents, but it's the ninety-one dollars that has put me past what I'm authorized to spend."

I start to leave. The salesman shakes my hand.

"Deal," he says. "Write the check."

Some may say my shrewd buying tactics saved our marriage. I say the whale belched in the nick of time.

He Tarzan, Me Jane.
We Friends?

Becky Freeman

"Honey," I sighed as I leaned against the couch. "I feel so ugly and old lately."

"Oh, I know how you feel," Scott started in. "My knees ache, my hair's thinning, my teeth hurt…"

"You just don't get it, do you?" I interrupted.

"Get what?" he asked, bewilderment clouding his eyes.

"Look, when I say, 'I feel so ugly,' that's your big cue to say something nice about me. 'I feel ugly' means 'I need a compliment.'"

Scott shook his head. "I get so confused. I thought 'I feel ugly' was my cue to be empathetic."

I rolled my eyes in exasperation. "Okay, let's go over it again. If I say, 'Honey, I just bounced a check' or 'Scott, I just ran into the mailbox'—that's when I want empathy. But if I tell you I feel old and ugly…"

"You want a compliment!"

"Yes!"

"Refresh me again: What kind of compliment?"

"'You grow more beautiful every year' is always a safe bet."

"Oh," Scott replied thoughtfully. "You grow more beautiful every year."

"Thank you," I replied.

Mastering the art of communication with the opposite sex is no easy trick. It takes years of practice, but I believe it begins by accepting two basic truths: "men are not women" and "women are not men." As you can see from the above conversation, Scott has his work cut out for him as he struggles to live with his "wife in an understanding way." I'm also trying my best these days to understand men. Recently, I received a list of "49 Facts About Men" from an alert "Marriage 9-1-1" reader. They were credited to comedienne Rita Rudner. I offer a sampling below with my blessings (and a very wide grin):

- Men like to barbecue. Men will cook if danger is involved.
- Men look nerdy in black socks and sandals.
- Men hate to hear, "We need to talk about our relationship." These seven words could strike fear in the heart of even General Schwarzkopf.
- Men are sensitive in strange ways. If a man builds a fire and the last log doesn't burn, he'll take it personally.
- Most women are introspective: "Am I in love? Am I emotionally and creatively fulfilled?" Most men are outrospective: "Did my team win? How's my car?"

"You grow more beautiful every year" is always a safe bet."

- Men who listen to classical music tend not to spit.
- Men are afraid of eyelash curlers. I sleep with one under my pillow, instead of a gun.
- Men have higher body temperature than women—men are like portable heaters that snore.
- Men love watches with multiple functions. My husband has one that's a combination address book, telescope and piano.
- Men would still really like to own a train set.

Before someone protests, "This is stereotyping men!" may I quickly interject that I believe the third step toward peace between the sexes involves enjoying a good-natured laugh at ourselves. How important it is for us to step back from the Marriage Picture and find humor again in our differences.

I don't know about you, but I'm sick of the ugly battles between men and women. "Male chauvinist!" the feminists accuse. "Male basher!" the men shout back. I long for men and women to come together, to view our differences with smiles of appreciation and curiosity—even though the reality is we'll never completely understand each other.

One of the things I love about watching old movies is that I get to peek in at a time when men were men, women were women, and relationships weren't micro-analyzed. I recently watched an old Walt Disney version of *Swiss Family Robinson*. I couldn't help but notice an underlying simplicity, a sweetness between John Robinson and his wife.

I loved the scene where John invites his mate, for the first time, to come and see the tree house he built. As they climb up the ladder together, John's face goes from proud man/survivor to vulnerable little boy—as he waits, wondering what his lady will think of his handiwork. With one sharp word, she could cut his heart in two. She teases him gently at first, but finally lets go—as tears fall freely in appreciation of her husband's efforts. I saw in John, as I see in most men, a basic, wonderful, almost instinctual desire to nurture and protect women—to make them happy. It's just that men have a rather clumsy way of showing this at times. (I find it helps to remember most men are just grown-up little boys with mortgages.)

So we have some differences. Guys barbecue. Gals sauté.

Men wear nerdy socks. Women wear old robes.

Men build with Lincoln Logs. Women decorate Dream Houses.

He Tarzan. Me Jane.

But since it gets awfully lonely clinging so tightly to our own vines—whadaya say we swing over to the same tree and make friends again?

L♥ve Must Be Sh♥w-and-Tell

Tim Wildmon

I once heard a speaker on relationships say what men mean by good communication are the headlines and what women look for in quality communication is the fine print.

What is it about the male sex that makes us have a difficult time expressing—or at least verbalizing—ourselves? Generally, we have trouble with everything from the small things, like what happened at work, to larger matters such as love and affection toward other people. Often, we even have trouble expressing ourselves to God.

One night my then five-year-old son Wesley and I were lying in bed as the family was winding down—ever so slowly—for bedtime. I don't want to mislead you into thinking our family is superreligious—because we're not—but one thing we do try to do each evening is pray with the children. We don't always make it there, but when we do I normally ask Wriley, our daughter, to

I told him his Pa Pa Wildmon was an ordained minister of the gospel and that he had no choice but to pray at least seven minutes in King James English.

go first, then Wesley, then Mom, and then me. Well, Wesley's usual response to my request for him to pray is a low, barely audible, "I don't want to." (And you thought I was going to quote him as saying something sweet and profound.) No real reason, just, "I don't want to."

One night I told him his Pa Pa Wildmon was an ordained minister of the gospel and that he—Wesley—had no choice but to pray at least seven minutes in King James English. To which Wesley responded, "I'm onlyth fiveth and my vocabulary is not that goodeth." I letteth him slideth that night. (By the way, this King James guy. Did he die of cotton mouth or did he choke to death on his own swollen tongue? Nobody can talk like that without carrying around bottled water.)

Now Wesley doesn't mind holding hands and he doesn't mind closing his eyes but he, unlike Wriley who can pray for everybody and everything, amen, doesn't like verbalizing a prayer. But then, when I call home he doesn't like talking on the phone either, unlike Wriley who will talk about everybody and everything, amen. I've found, with rare exception, males are like this.

Do you remember calling home from college? Who was the one that wanted to talk most and ask lots of questions? It was Mom, right? Dads generally just want to know if the oil has been changed in the car and if you are studying. One is a yes/no question and the other is relative. Until the grades arrive home anyway.

I am this way with my wife Alison on the phone. She wants to ask me about this, that, and the other, and she wants some detailed information. She wants to know what I think, what's best, my reaction, and my feelings. To which I usually respond, "I don't know, babe, do what you want."

Often when she knows I'm not half paying attention, she'll put me on the spot. "What did I just say to you?" she'll ask.

Usually I try to piece together something which comes out as convoluted nonsense. It could go something like this:

"You said go pick up Wesley at church Thursday night at eleven o'clock after gymnastics and bring home seventy dollars worth of pizzas from Taco Bell."

To which she responds, "I knew you weren't listening to me. You need help. Now, Tim, I can't run this family all by myself, so you better listen to me or it's going to be unpleasant for all of us, especially you. Do you hear me?"

To which I reply, "I don't know, babe, do what you want." (Ha! Ha! This is a joke, ladies. Please, lighten up.)

But on this particular night Wesley and I were alone for a couple of minutes and I asked him if we could pray. When I asked him if he would pray, he said yes. *We're making progress here,* I thought. So we both closed our eyes and I held his hand. Waiting, I said, "You can go first." He squinted and said softly, "Dear God, um (ten seconds of silence here), um, dear God, um...I don't really have anything to say." So I gave him a few simple words, which he repeated, we said good night, and off to sleep he went.

For some reason it seems boys and men find it difficult to verbally express affection and love to others. Wesley will one day outgrow his inability to say a prayer, but we all, especially men, need to get past whatever it is that keeps us from telling those around us how we feel about them. Yes, we need to demonstrate love to our wives, our family, and to God—but they also need to hear it from us and hear it often.

The way I see it, if we can slap each other on the rear end after a great play on the football field or baseball diamond, often in front of thousands of people and sometimes on national television without an ounce of shame or embarrassment, we ought to be able to tell those who matter most how we feel, right? In fact, most of these men get paid millions of dollars to—among other things—pat each other on the buttocks. (Not to carry this out too far, but you know you've played a good game if your bottom's sore when the game's over. The better you play, the more slaps on the rear you get from your teammates.) So, what about it, men?

Say it with me, guys, say it out loud, "How 'bout them Cowboys!" Wait a minute, that just came out of nowhere, let me try again. Let's say it together, "I love you." That's it, say it again, only louder and pretend you're looking your wife, child, or your own dad right in the eye. "I love you." You're catching on. Now you can send me the money you were going to send Gary Smalley for those videotapes.

How often do we tell God that we love Him? Do we demonstrate that love with our lives? How often do we tell our wives that we love them, and show that love to be genuine with our actions? The same with our children and others around us.

Jesus set the standard for us. He told His disciples He loved them and then He proved it. Indeed, words are cheap if they are not backed up with actions. But then again, there are no more powerful words in the world than, "I love you." So let me encourage you to do as Wesley will be doing in school this fall: play a little show-and-tell. In your case, try doing it with those you love and care for.

Chapter 8

it's my body and
i'll cry if i want to—

weighty
hum♥R

The 30-Day Diet

The 30-day diet is quite popular—that's the one people are going to start in about 30 days.

—FROM OVER THE HILL & ON A ROLL, BOB PHILLIPS

Absolutely Flabulous

Ken Davis

When I turned forty, a strange thing happened to my metabolism. It stopped. Now all I have to do is *look* at the fat grams listed on the nutrition label of a candy bar, and they're automatically sucked into me. I know the body is supposed to be a temple, but does it have to be the Mormon Tabernacle? I'd be just as happy resembling a small country church.

How did this happen? I was so skinny in high school that I wasn't safe in a stiff breeze. I didn't want anyone to see me in a bathing suit because of my toothpick arms. I wore a towel around my shoulders until I was safely underwater. Dragging that towel around, no wonder I had trouble swimming.

I tried to gain weight with exercise. I faithfully did my push-ups, my sit-ups, and my throw-ups. I even tried the isometrics theory of muscle development. Isometric exercise consists of tightening every muscle in your body and holding it that way until you change colors.

I even tried isometrics in church. I placed both hands together as if I were praying, then pressed with all my might. My face turned beet-red. I looked up to see the pastor staring directly at me. He wasn't speaking, just looking at me with that "what would Jesus do?" look. My mom and dad were looking at me too. After the service, they did more than just look at me. They touched me.

Once I passed out while doing isometrics. I took a deep breath and tensed up every muscle in my body; I turned red. Then everything else turned red. Then it all went black. It's true that I didn't gain one ounce of muscle, but those thirty seconds of unconsciousness gave me a nice little break from the tension of trying to gain weight.

I also tried the technique of eating. My mother would pack a school lunch, including an entire loaf of bread with a jar of jelly and one of peanut butter. I'd come home with an empty lunch pail, toothpick arms, and peanut-butter breath that would have offended even an elephant.

When I entered college, the hormones finally kicked in. The exercise I was doing began to pay off. My shoulders suddenly broadened; real muscles began to pop up and stand proudly on my bones.

Unfortunately, the eating began to pay off too. Fresh layers of fat obscured any muscular definition that might lie beneath them. I traded in the loaves of bread for Cinnabuns, summer sausage, and pasta. By the time I reached the age of twenty-five, I tipped the scales at 230—most of it seemingly in my face and thighs. The face is a bad place to carry an extra fifty pounds. My neck disappeared and my cheeks puffed out until it looked as if I were storing nuts for the winter. I couldn't run well because my thighs impeded each other.

I hadn't seen my shoes in over six months. It was time to do something.

My first diet began a roller-coaster ride that runs on into the present day. I tried everything in the book. I drank a popular fluid diet that tasted like chocolate gravel, and I lost fifty-one pounds. But you can't live on that stuff. As soon as I went back to real eating, the weight came back.

I tried the Atkins Diet. I restricted myself to meat, fat, and protein and avoided all carbohydrates. The word *carbohydrate* comes from a Latin word meaning "tastes very good." So for six months I ate only high-protein foods with no taste. I lost no weight and drove my cholesterol over the 300 mark. The doctor told me I could market my blood for motor oil.

In the midst of this mess, I decided to have the fat content of my body analyzed by being weighed underwater. I already knew I was too fat—now I was going to pay someone to tell me how much too fat I was. This near-death experience supposedly enables the doctor to determine the exact percentage of fat in your body. You lose a certain amount of weight quickly but painfully. It comes out of your wallet.

The theory goes like this: Muscle and bone sink, fat floats, and money talks. If you give seventy-five dollars to someone with a white coat and a supreme-being air about him, he'll weigh you on dry land, then weigh you underwater. Then he subtracts one figure from the other and determines what percentage of your body is fat. For example, if I

The word carbohydrate comes from a
Latin word meaning "tastes very good."

weigh 230 on dry land and 30 underwater, then 200 pounds floated.

That means eighty-seven percent of my weight is fat. I am a human bobber. On the other hand, if I weigh 230 pounds on dry land and 200 underwater, then eighty-seven percent of my body weight is muscle and bone. I'm a human anchor, struggling to get off the bottom of the pool.

On the day of my test, the supreme being in the white coat lightened my wallet by seventy-five dollars. That was fifty percent of my net worth. If only he could have eliminated fifty percent of my net weight.

A huge crane extended out over the deep end of a swimming pool. Hanging from the crane was a large swing: the scale. The supreme being's assistant strapped me into the swing, then the white-coated one maneuvered it out over the pool. "Let all the air out of your body," he commanded. I started laughing. As the only male member of my family, I had never been encouraged to let all the air out of my body.

Apparently the great white one had a sense-of-humor content of less than one percent. He gruffly commanded me to breathe out. It was no use reminding him that God didn't intend for us to breathe out before going underwater. He designed us to suck air into our bodies. This is so we can live.

I breathed out until only pitiful little squeaks were coming from my lungs. The swing was suddenly plunged into the water. They can't read the scale accurately until the chair stops bouncing.

Do you know how long it took for the chair to stop bouncing? Let me tell you. In my oxygen-deprived state I thought sure I saw Jesus at the end of a long white tunnel gesturing for me to come to the light. My grandmother was there too, beckoning. I began to move toward the warm glow when I was suddenly jerked from the water. As I gasped for air the light faded, Grandma disappeared, and the white coat proclaimed, "Yep, you're fat!"

"I want a second opinion!" I sputtered, gulping for breath.

"You're ugly too!" he smirked. Just like that I had my diagnosis, I had my second opinion, and I was out seventy-five dollars.

If you still insist on knowing the fat content of your body, I've developed a method that won't cost you a cent. Next time you get out of the shower, grab a stopwatch and stand in front of a full-length mirror totally naked. Start the watch and stamp your foot on the floor as hard as you can. When stuff stops moving, punch the watch and check the time.

I'm down to two days, three hours, and six minutes.

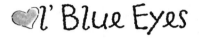

'l' Blue Eyes

Luci Swindoll

Not long ago I was in a local bookstore, investigating one of the many new books on dieting, and discovered there was an entire Diet Section in the store. It was full of overweight people, lethargically pulling the volumes from the shelves and leafing through pages of information pertaining to newer and better ways to take off inches and pounds. A few were talking about that four-letter word which seems to dominate the English language—DIET.

And that isn't all. In the aisle next to the one where we were solving the problems of the avoirdupois, there were three ladies poring over a new book on exercise...running, I believe it was. They looked fabulous. Tan. Thin. Sleek. Perfect. Yet, they confessed to one another their desire to run at least one more mile next time...to get an even richer tan...to work out at the Club more faithfully. All of our team in the Diet Section were trying not to listen as they rehearsed their goals, since they, no doubt, were already outdistancing us in every way. I simply resumed munching my Almond Joy.

After locating the book I was seeking, I picked it up and started toward the cash register. On my way, I walked through an aisle labeled MENTAL HEALTH. These publications ranged from books on transcendental meditation to a volume entitled *Mental Gymnastics—Exercising While You Wait.* The person holding a copy of that appeared as though he were. His eyes were closed and I was certain he was either in a trance or not among the living, when suddenly, his eyes popped open and he realized I was looking straight at him. "Oh, I'm not doing a gymnastic," he said. "My contacts are killing me and I was trying to rest my eyes." We exchanged a few lines about the price we all pay for vanity, then we parted, the same strangers we were when we met.

On my way back to work I started thinking about all the books that must have been written on health. Countless thousands. And not only books! Good health is touted on television, radio, and in films. National magazines are replete with recommended ways to be healthy and stay healthy. Of course, we all know why. Health is a treasure and fitness is an enviable state for anyone. When we have healthy minds, bodies, and spirits, we have personal assurance that we will be strong enough and sound enough to live our lives fully, coping effectively with life's problems rather than being the victim of them.

But few things in life are ideal. Realistically, therefore, we must admit that the living of daily life produces all sorts of inner factions and tensions that can manifest themselves in physical pain, mental anguish, and spiritual depression. Surely, no one has trouble admitting that! That's the way things are. But...as we grasp good principles for healthy living, as we learn that we can prevent certain ills from occurring by simply using our heads, and as we realize that God provides marvelous promises for His children to claim and rely on when we are not well, the prognosis for a sound and healthy life becomes brighter and more probable.

However, to achieve this kind of thinking and to live on this plane, one must DO certain things to provide physical well-being, and BE certain ways to maintain the homeostasis required for one's psyche. I have hanging on the wall of my office a clever saying that reminds me of this need for balance between doing and being:

TO DO IS TO BE

—Plato

TO BE IS TO DO

—Sartre

TO DO BE DO BE DO

—Sinatra

I think "ol' Blue Eyes" has the best outlook of all, don't you?

Rej♥ice!

Sheila Walsh

"I think it would be a good idea if you could lose a few pounds before the tour begins," my manager suggested gingerly.

Yeah, and I think it would be a good idea if you grew your hair back! I thought to myself.

Bill Latham meant well. I was going on the tour of a lifetime supporting British megastar Cliff Richard. Cliff has never been well known in America, but in the rest of the world he has sold more singles than The Beatles, The Rolling Stones, and The Who all put together. (And no, those are not Southern gospel quartets!) As well as being a successful pop star, Cliff is also a very committed Christian. Once a year he would do a tour for a British relief charity called Tear Fund, and this time I was the opening act.

I was humiliated by Bill's "suggestion," but I'll admit I needed to lose weight. I don't mean I was huge. You couldn't have shown

I was weighed in by a skinny thing who looked like her clothes had been sprayed on her tiny frame.

Ben Hur on my posterior, but I definitely fell into the "chunky" category. I had tried for ages to lose the twenty pounds that I tucked into my jeans and under my sweater; but they were clingy little pounds and reluctant to be evicted from their cozy, well-fed home.

"I've tried to diet," I whined pathetically. "My pastor told me that if I would just carry all of my diet books up and down the stairs a few times I'd never have a weight problem again."

"I have a plan," Bill said with a look of confidence.

My heart sank.

"I'm enrolling you in a clinic in London for two weeks. They will exercise you and put you on a strict diet and work wonders." He beamed. "You'll be a new woman!"

Good grief! I thought.

"All you have to do is stick with the program. Will you do that?"

"Oh, yes," I said with all the fervor of an alcoholic with a fifth of Scotch hidden in her sweater.

When I arrived at the "clinic" (i.e., fat farm), I was weighed in by a skinny thing who looked like her clothes had been sprayed on to emphasize her tiny frame. I had to keep my mouth firmly clamped so I wouldn't blurt out what was on the tip of my tongue: "Listen, Bones, if it wasn't for people like me, you'd be out of a job!"

For the next two weeks, Bones and her friends wrapped me and pummeled me and starved me till I looked like a leftover turkey at the homeless shelter on Thanksgiving. Then came D-Day. I think of it as "Black Tuesday." I stood on the scale and could have shot the little traitor. I had gained four pounds!

That's just one of the humiliating moments in my history. I hated myself. I was so ashamed that I had no willpower. I felt ugly and unlovable. I imagined when people looked at me they saw a fat, unattractive girl because that's what I saw in the bathroom mirror…if I turned on the light.

But Christ didn't die so I'd continue to feel rotten about myself! Ephesians 2:13 tells me, "But now in Christ Jesus you who once were far away have been brought near through the blood of Christ." I spent many years as a believer, knowing I was pardoned for my sin but keeping a distance even from God because I didn't find myself worth loving. Every magazine I read showed images so far removed from my reality that I despaired of ever feeling worthy—until I was invited to a party with Cliff Richard and realized that all the so-called "beautiful people" were empty if they had no relationship with Christ. I sat and listened as Cliff shared his faith with people whose faces were well known to me. I watched as tears streamed down perfect makeup onto designer dresses. I realized how I had bought into the lies and despair of the world. I asked God to forgive me. I didn't need to be a "new woman" according to the world's ideas. I was already loved completely by God, as the woman I was.

When you look in a mirror, what do you see? Do you zero in on a crooked nose, a blemish, a sagging jaw, tired eyes packing their own bags? Have whole parts of your body moved to a new neighborhood? I encourage you as a fellow traveler to cherish and celebrate the gift of grace that calls you to draw near, to let go of your obsession with the shell of your life, and to fall more in love with Jesus. As those who have been drawn close to the heart of God by the embrace of Christ, you and I have the best reason of all to rejoice. Because God is near—no matter what.

D♥ Plastic Surge♥ns Take Visa?

Kathy Peel

"Mommy, did you know your legs are lumpy like cottage cheese?"

Six-year-old James broadcast his observation to the entire shallow end of the swimming pool. Even the lifeguard glanced down our way to see if he could spot this strange phenomenon. I just smiled at him and the twenty-something mothers whose toned and tanned bodies were posed poolside. I'd like to see what they look like at forty, I thought snidely as I slipped into the pool hoping to hide my prominent thighs. Nevertheless, I had a feeling it was going to be a long summer.

James's comment spurred me on. Weight control is a constant battle for me, but I'm committed to keep fighting. I sincerely believe God wants us to take care of ourselves—to look and feel our best. And I feel better about myself when I take care of my body. So that afternoon I decided it was time to take inventory—from the top down. I wanted to know just what I had to work with. I locked the bedroom door and started my evaluation at my dressing table. As I traced the lines and crevices across my face, my hopes that the kids had overlaid a map of the Mississippi and its tributaries on the makeup mirror vanished. My twice-a-day Queen Esther routine was obviously not working. The cabinet full of anti-age, nonwrinkle, rejuvenating creams had delivered minimal results, and I was now codependent on Oil of Olay.

I then mustered up every ounce of courage within me and stood stark naked in front of a full-length mirror. It was a scary sight. Twenty years and three children since my wedding day, and my chest gave new meaning to the word "swags." Not only that, they were swags for a very small drape. Suddenly the term "breast augmentation" took on new significance. I calculated that if I clipped coupons for the next nine years and pocketed the money, I could save enough to have one breast enlarged. I decided that an uplifting padded bra would be a much more balanced approach and less risky.

Glancing down at my tummy and thighs was quite a shock to my system as well. Why, pray tell, was I not born during the Renaissance when plump, pear-shaped bodies were in vogue? I could have easily been the centerfold for *Seventeenth Century Woman* magazine. But no...I have to live at the end of the twentieth century when anyone wider than a popsicle stick qualifies for a liquid diet commercial.

As I continued my evaluation, I confessed my whining and decided to take a spiritual approach to the problem of getting back into shape. I wondered what God would think of liposuction. I searched my Bible and found the verse "woe...to them that give suck..." Now I know that verse from Matthew 24 wasn't written about liposuction. But it made sense in a quirky sort of way. So I decided I'd best try a different angle. Maybe a girdle would work—a silent one that wouldn't screech when my thighs rub together.

I finished the assessment with a panoramic view of my hair style—which had the appearance of a heavy traffic path in shag carpet. My kids called it my "matted poodle" look. When I asked my hair stylist to give me a new young look, I didn't know that to create this "carefree" style I'd have to spend forty-five minutes using a diffuser, three types of hair picks, two sizes of round brushes, hot rollers, duckbill clips, mousse, and spritzer, only to look as if I'd just survived a tornado.

As much as I hated to admit it, when I scanned the perimeter of my middle-aged body, I knew I was dealing with a long-range project. With determination not to let this get me down, I got dressed. I heard a knock on my door. "Mom, are you okay in there?" I opened the door and tried to bolster my self-image by fishing for a compliment. "Guys, did I ever tell you I was once in a beauty contest with Cybill Shepherd?" They rolled their eyes and responded, "You've told us that story at least twenty times, and we still want to send it to *Ripley's Believe It or Not.*"

After threatening to discontinue their allowance, I indignantly reminded them that I take care of my body. I sucked in my stomach and continued, "I'm looking pretty sharp for a forty-one-year-old woman. I can still get into most of my size-eight skirts and, lucky for you, I haven't dipped into your college fund to get my eyelids done."

I thought for sure they would fall prostrate at my feet and call me blessed. Instead they dug into their repertoire of fam-

Maybe a girdle would work—a silent one that wouldn't screech when my thighs rub together.

ily barbs and started in with flabby-arm-waving jokes and "Did the Flood occur before or after you were born?" comments. John philosophically added, "Gosh, I bet I'm the only kid on earth with a mom whose hair color and skin color both come out of a bottle. Mom, give it up. It's a little late for the California-girl look."

I was thankful I'd passed the stage of allowing my children's jokes to determine my self-esteem. I played along with them and we had a good laugh. But inwardly I knew it wasn't getting any easier to keep the makeup from caking in the creases and the pounds from creeping up on the scales.

I find nothing wrong with wanting to look nice and maximize the "equipment" God gave me. I am the King of kings' royal representative on earth, and I want to represent him in the loveliest way I can. I also want my family to be proud of me. And I want to be my best for myself too. When I feel good about how I look and feel, I'm free to love and give myself to others. I accomplish a lot more too.

"Every little bit helps." My children hate it when I say that—especially when we're playing Monopoly. While they're holding out for the big properties—waiting to be able to put hotels on Boardwalk and Park Place, I'm stockpiling the cheaper ones. I save the small bits of rent money they owe when they land on my houses in the "low-rent district," as they put it. But guess who usually wins? I do, because all the little deals add up to a big win at the end.

I think the same principle holds true for dieting and taking care of our bodies—every little bit helps. But as we each strive in our own way to make the most of our personal appearance, let us never forget what's most important—that it is God's will for each of us to become like Jesus Christ, the loveliest creature of all.

the family that
laughs together...

"Your Father's Side"

The young boy had never seen his grandmother. Then she came to visit.

"Are you really my grandmother?" the boy asked.

"Yes," she said. "On your father's side."

He leaned closer to her. "I can tell you right now, you're on the losing side."

—FROM MAKE MY DAY!, ROBERT SAVAGE

Vulcan Child Care

Dan N. "Max" Mayhew

I regret to inform you that whatever child rearing method you used, or are currently using is probably obsolete. My parents were assured in a book called *Baby and Child Care*, by some guy named Dr. Spock, that there was a foolproof way of mass producing a generation of premium grade adults. Unfortunately, all they got from his method was the "sixties," wherein thousands of young people abandoned the military industrial complex (which was very popular with parents at that time) and went out to develop a social conscience. This meant that they would pay tuition at a local college—better yet, have their parents pay—then refuse to go to classes until the government agreed to abolish Vietnam. Finally, everybody under the age of thirty piled into brightly colored VW buses and went to Woodstock to sing songs about social conscience until they could afford to buy a haircut and a BMW. Then they became what sociologists call "Boomers."

Meanwhile, their parents had gotten angry enough to hurl Spock into outer space, where it was discovered that he was really from another planet and thought humans were illogical. This is when the term, "duh...," was introduced into the English language. Having just raised the aforementioned generation, parents didn't need an alien to tell them that humans, particularly children, were illogical. The question on the mind of most parents as they tossed *Baby and Child Care* into the recycling bin was, "Why didn't he include a chapter on the 'Vulcan death grip?'" Knowing how to hold a hostile alien or a recalcitrant child by the back of the neck with your thumb and forefinger until they became compliant or until the next commercial, whichever came first, would have come in handy in the sixties.

After the failure of Spock's method of raising children, parents in the seventies called in child development experts [EX'•PERT, *noun*. From "ex-" that is, "a has-been" and "spurt" that is, "a drip under pressure"] to work on a new way to raise the perfect child even *without* the Vulcan death grip. To do this, the experts initiated what is called "research," wherein highly trained people in white lab coats and carrying clipboards followed randomly selected normal American families around and took notes called "data."

After the data was collected, or the experts were arrested for stalking, it was brought back to the lab for "analysis," which means that the data was copied into neat rows on 8½ x 11 college-ruled paper until it turned into what experts call a "theory." This theory was then scientifically tested in a controlled environment and documented on film that was eventually released to the public in the form of *The Brady Bunch,* which clearly indicated the need for more research.

Finally, after years of painstaking trial and error, one of the experts, exhausted and irritable at the end of a frustrating day in the lab, went home to his equally irritable family and hollered at the kids, "Just be quiet and go to your room!" This caused what psychologists call, "an 'ah-ha!' moment," in which the expert became inspired to invent the premier disciplinary method of the '80s, the TIME-OUT (Reg. U.S. Patent #4,689,852).

This is how it works: When a child is unruly, merely interrupt him in the midst of whatever unruly activity he is doing and, in a controlled tone of voice, say "TIME-OUT!" which is a code word that means, "Go sit on the sofa and act like you've been paralyzed by a Vulcan death grip!" (Judy and I tried this approach without success. Our kids would sit on the couch and fondly remember how much more exciting whatever they did wrong was than sitting on the couch, then devise detailed plans to do it again without getting caught.)

By the end of the '80s, parents, like the generation before them, became skeptical. There were some unexpected side effects from TIME-OUT!, namely that TIME-OUT! had become a way of life for many children. This was probably because the kids were sent to their rooms, which were fully equipped with a Gameboy™ and/or a small television on which they could watch guests of Maury Povich stick balloons in their nose. In desperation, parents tried to reverse the effects by saying something like, "Time-in!" or, "Get a job!" but it was too late. By the early nineties, there were thousands of twenty-somethings still in TIME-OUT! with apparently no way to turn it off.

By the early nineties, there were thousands of twenty-somethings still in TIME-OUT! with apparently no way to turn it off.

This is a serious situation. If we can't get the next generation out of TIME-OUT! we will have no way of funding the military industrial complex which will cause the collapse of social security. That's why scientific "Boomers," nearing retirement age, have been spending lots of money to set up vast arrays of radio telescopes. They are scanning the heavens, awaiting the historic moment when intelligible radio signals are beamed across the galaxy: *Chapter 12: The Vulcan Death Grip.*

Tuning In
Nancy Moser

"Ga!"

My mother pounced on the word. "Come quick! Emily said 'Grandma!'"

I finished mixing Emily's rice cereal with some formula.

"Nancy! Come in here! She said it!"

I dutifully went into the living room to hear proof that my firstborn was a prodigy. Mom had Emily seated in her infant seat and was cajoling her with animated facial expressions.

"Come on, sweetie," she said. "You can do it. Say 'Grand-ma.'"

I tucked a bib under Emily's chin. "Mom, she's too little. She can't say 'grandma.'"

"Maybe not all of it, but she—"

"So she said part of it?" I asked. "As in 'gram'?"

"Not exactly."

"'Gam'?"

"Not exactly—"

"I'm running out of letters," I said.

Mom looked at me disgustedly. "She said 'ga.' She looked right at me and said 'ga.' And she smiled."

Actually, Emily was probably saying, "Golly gee, won't this lady ever leave me alone?"

"She says 'phfkjz' too," I said. "If you can tell me what that means, I'll get you a job with the United Nations."

My mother squared her shoulders and proceeded to feed Emily. "You don't have to believe me," she said. "But Emily and I know what she said."

It's odd how we are so eager for our kids to talk. We don't realize we're going to spend the rest of their childhoods telling them "Shh!" The key is: if we teach them how to talk, we have to teach them how to be quiet. I taught Emily this rule when she was five years old and we were riding in the car. I can remember the exact intersection where it happened....

Emily was rambling on—and on—about kindergarten, what she wanted to be for Halloween, the offenses of her two-year-old brother, Carson, and wondering if we called autumn "fall" because the leaves fell off the trees. Yet when Emily asked questions, she didn't pause long enough for me to answer. She was already zipping on to another subject. It was not a discussion. It was a monologue. It was exhausting keeping up with the workings of her little mind. It soon became apparent that whatever popped into her head popped out of her mouth. To be truthful, since she wasn't concerned with my involvement (and since it would have been difficult to get a word in anyway), while she rambled, I visited my own mental list of errands, schedules, and—

"But Emily and I know what she said." "You don't have to believe me," she said.

There was a moment of silence. Its sudden existence was shocking. I looked at Emily. She looked at me, her forehead furrowed.

"What's wrong?" I asked.

She sighed deeply. "I can't keep talking all the time. It makes me tired."

What? "You don't *have* to talk all the time," I said.

"I *don't?*"

I shook my head. "We can ride without saying a word," I said hopefully. "Or you can listen."

"To what?"

"To me. To what's going on outside. To what's going on inside. To the air rushing by."

"Wow," she said. "I'm so glad."

I have no idea where Emily got the notion she was expected to keep the air filled with words. I'm a talkative person, but even I take a breath once in awhile and I actually enjoy extended moments of silence. There are times to talk and times to—

Emily's misconception made me wonder how many times we think we have to talk at God in a never-ending banter. Do we wait for the answers to our questions? If we're not interested in his involvement—if we make it too hard for him to get a word in—he might just tune us out. We need to remember Emily's lesson: We don't need to talk all the time.

Sometimes, we need to listen. To each other. To what's going on outside. To what's going on inside. To the air rushing by.

Who knows? The air may be full of God's whispering voice, calling our name. Or maybe just telling us "Shh."

The T♥ni
Dennis Swanberg

Do you remember Sucrets? Not many of us ever took one of those elusive throat lozenges, but we can sure remember things that were stored in the boxes long after the lozenges were gone. A Sucrets box was a multifaceted thing. Our family had one that was mainly used to store bobby pins; it only came forth at a special time in our life—when Mama got a Toni!

Mama periodically saved up to buy a Toni home-permanent kit. She got so excited when she purchased one at the supermarket. She was pumped! It was a monumental moment for Mama.

Her getting a Toni was likened in the Swanberg family to her being the winner on the fifties television show *Queen for a Day*. It was Mama's new lease on life. It was her moment in the sun and our moment of nasal dismay. That stuff stank!

It was an event that was precipitated by many phone calls to aunts, grandparents, sisters, and friends. It was almost newsworthy in the local *Grit* magazine. And it was the catalyst for Mama's disposition for the next couple of months.

We would pray, "Lord Jesus, give us a good Toni for the family's sake. If Mama's not happy, nobody's happy."

On some Toni adventures, we traveled to Grandpa and Grandma Johnson's house in the country. Grandma Bell would administer the Toni on the front porch, next to the old church bench. All of the Toni paraphernalia would be laid on the church bench, but not to rest.

We kids usually sat out in the cotton field on a terrace and watched. This was a sight that I must explain.

Grandma always began by washing Mama's hair in a big white porcelain pan with a red rim, the one we kids were bathed in when we were babies. After slinging Mama's hair back, Grandma twisted it to wring it out. Then out came the comb. Grandma pulled it through Mama's hair, taking out the tangles. We watched Mama wince, but she was willing to endure the pain for the excitement of getting a Toni.

Grandma started with a strand of hair, poured on the milky solution, and then put a square of toilet tissue on Mama's hair. Next she rolled that strand of hair around a pencil and slid the curl down to Mama's head. With two bobby pins from the Sucrets box, she pinned Mama's new Toni curl down!

We were waiting for the Toni bottle; that stuff stank to high heaven. It was not a sweet aroma to the Lord. But Grandma seemed to enjoy the smell. When she took that bottle and poured it on Mama's hair, the ozone layer visibly changed. We cringed, Mama held her nose, and Grandma inhaled. Even the mud daubers took off from their nest under the eaves of the porch!

We loved watching those mud daubers get out of the way.

Their formation was, *Everyone on your own; abandon mission.* They weren't the Blue Angels, but they were the Flying Daubers, reminiscent of the Flying Tigers of World War II!

We kids qualified Mama's Toni's by how many mud daubers were affected when Grandma dabbed on that stinky, milky, murky liquid.

That day on Grandma's porch, Mama's Toni was a nine-dauber 'do. Others ranged between four and seven, but that day was the one and only nine-dauber 'do.

Those were the days. Life's joys were there for all of us: Mama, Grandma, we kids, and the mud daubers.

We enjoyed the elementary things of life. Looking back, I realize that those times were memorable and noteworthy. They were our basic education before entering the upper-level courses of life.

Mama was satisfied with a Toni, whereas moms today want a nine-dauber special at a nine-chair salon. Who knows how they do hair today? It's all done behind closed doors. In those days, it was done on the porch. We were family, and we all experienced it together.

Mama even went to the grocery store with her hair in pins to show off her impending moment of glory. Her hair would soon unfold and hold. We would be blessed, and Mama would be transformed.

Now when I open my medicine cabinet and see a Sucrets box, I remember those Toni moments and am reminded of how good life was, is, and will be. Every family needs a box of memories.

Teen Hair Disaster

Dan N. "Max" Mayhew

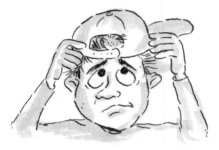

If we had it to do over, I think we would have named our teenage son something other than Benjamin. I think a peaceful name like "Lake" or maybe "Sky" might have been better. As it is, we named our third born child before realizing that "Benjamin" has biblical roots and means, "son of the right hand."

This turned out to be a kind of prophecy regarding Ben's learning style. Based on our experience, a modern translation might be, "son of the wooden spoon" or "son of the twelve-hour time out.'"

In practice, this means that if he has decided to see what it's like to beat his head against a rock, he will not be convinced that it's a bad thing until he sees blood—sometimes, not even then.

This is what the *LEARNED ONES* call a "kinesthetic learner." Normal parents call it "active" or "busy."

When the kid is a youngster, this means the parents should give leeway for exploration, but seek to be firm and consistent. When the kid is a teenager, it means that the parents should *seek justice!*

Last week, justice visited our house. To be specific, it visited Ben's head. He had made the acquaintance of a young lady who offered to cut his hair. Apparently, she wasn't completely satisfied with Ben "as is," so she decided that with a little creative shaping and styling she could make him look like Leonardo DiCaprio. Ben, always eager to please as long as it isn't his parents, agreed to let her practice her art on his head.

I don't know what actually happened, but Ben gave me this account of a conversation he had with his best friend as they were leaving the scene. I'll do my best to translate.

Friend: "Dude, you better wear a hat."

Ben: "Whaddya talkin' about, dude?"

Friend: "Dude! She done jacked your head up *deep.*"

Ben: "Come on. Don't mess wit me, dude!"

Friend: "I'm not messin' witcha, dude, it's lookin' baaaad."

Moral of the story: Friends don't let friends get their hair cut by amateurs, no matter how good looking they are, er, dude.

When Ben got up the next morning nothing had changed for the better. Jill, my college student daughter, and her boyfriend, Sonny, who was sharing a room with Benjamin for the summer while working as an intern at the police department, knew what to expect. They were both up when Ben came home the night before. The rest of us were unaware.

"I noticed something weird, but I thought it was because I hadn't had my coffee."

"Did you see Ben's hair?" Jill asked in the kitchen as I pondered the paper.

"I noticed something weird, but I thought it was because I hadn't had my coffee."

We went into the living room where Ben was sitting dejectedly on the couch. His mother was clearly enjoying this. In Judy's mind this was *pay back time.*

"It looks like there was a flock of gerbils grazing on your head last night," she said.

To make things worse, Ben had some hair color the girl had bought for him so he could make his hair blonde. It was to be the *coup de grace.* It would attract all the more attention to his head, but she was expecting him to use it.

Jill considered the situation. "You could shorten it around the sides," she suggested.

"I can't change it," Ben protested. "Melanie thinks she did a good job."

"She won't remember. She was obviously intoxicated."

"You can't leave it like that," Sonny said. "I can use my trimmer to shorten it on the sides so it won't look so raggedy."

Sonny's hair is close-cropped, Marine-style. This clearly worried Ben. On the other hand, hair grows from the bottom so there wasn't much choice but to trim it. The result was a fairly close approximation of what's in style—with nubs on the sides and longer hair around the top of the head. It's just the opposite of my hair.

With the nicks and gouges mostly gone, Ben applied the hair color. I encouraged him to read the directions. A young friend of ours, whose hair color does not appear in nature unless you're a flower, had gone nearly bald from doing it wrong.

Nonetheless, the first application didn't seem to be working very well, so Ben decided to take another stab at it. The family went about its business and waited while he stalked the house with a towel around his head. There was the sound of Jill's hair dryer upstairs. The tension was palpable. We heard him come down the stairs and disappear in the bathroom to put on the finishing touches. Emerging a few minutes later, Ben stood apprehensively as we considered the effect.

"How does it look?" he asked finally.

Judy offered her analysis: "Like you moussed your hair with Cheez Whiz."

It was true. The color was supposed to be something like "Summer Sunshine," but looked more like "Kodak Yellow." It was either endure or get out the trimmer.

He endured.

A couple of days later, Judy went shopping at the supermarket where Ben works. When she went through the line the clerk recognized her. "How do you like Ben's hair?" she asked. Judy just smiled a satisfied smile.

Justice, sweet justice!

Chapter 10

amusing animals—

pet hum♥R

Signs

Entertaining signs found around the country...

- On a residential fence: Salesmen welcome. Dog food is expensive

- On a residential front door: Everyone on the premises is a vegetarian except the dog.

- On a veterinarian's door:
  Back in ten minutes. Sit. Stay.

—FROM ESPRESSO FOR YOUR SPIRIT: HOPE AND HUMOR FOR
POOPED OUT PARENTS, PAM VREDEVELT

Experiencing Dog

Chris Fabry

I have always hated listening to pet stories, especially when people go on and on about the utter cuteness of their little poochie. (By the way, I refuse to capitalize the name of a dog.)

In my view, the only good pet stories describe: (1) an animal saving a human's life, (2) a pet gnawing off its leg to survive, (3) a pet gnawing off a human's leg to save a person's life, or (4) a pet gnawing off a leg just for fun. Otherwise, don't tell me your pet story.

The worst pet stories are told by those who try to draw a spiritual parallel to life. I recall listening to one contemporary singer draw grand lessons from the life of a new puppy, and the disdain I felt as I thought, *Boy, I'll never do that!*

This was before we purchased pippen, our dog. Pippen (I have to capitalize the first word of a sentence, even if it's a dog's name) came to us highly recommended. The ad said something like, "Good with children, doesn't shed, gnaws at leg, and makes great chapter material in poignant, life-changing books." *That's the dog for me,* I thought, so we brought pippen home at the beginning of a hot summer, and he's been part of the family ever since.

One great spiritual lesson I've learned from the cute little thing (I'm really very sorry about this) is the value of contentment. We have a stake in the backyard and a leash attached to it that will travel in a fifteen-foot radius. It doesn't matter how much food or water pippen has in his dish, how many toys are in his area, or how much sleep the neighbors are trying to get, every time we put him outside, he runs to the end of the leash and paces back and forth, barking and whimpering.

This, of course, wears out the grass in that section of the yard. It also drives those inside the house crazy. "Shut your yap!" we scream affectionately. Hour after hour he paces and pants, straining to the edge of the well-worn path. The only thing that keeps him from the limits of his area is the presence of someone he loves. When one of us ventures into his circle, he jumps, delighted to have company.

I sat down beside him one day and thought deeply about my life. As pippen gnawed on my leg, I looked at my life and my leash. God has given me good things. I have a place to run filled with pleasures, but I'm always straining for more, barking and whining when I don't get something I think I need. I don't fully appreciate the things given me because I'm so focused on what's over there by the swing set or in the neighbor's yard.

But I'm different from pippen in an important way. This makes me sad. He is our dog. Our name and phone number are on his collar. Likewise, I am a child of God. I am a disciple and bear the name of Christ. But as I look closely at my life, my everyday yearnings are not focused on the Master. I don't strain at the end of my leash for him. Much of the time, I'm looking for things that ultimately will not satisfy.

This is the kind of spiritualizing you get in just about any book that includes pet stories, but now I kick into the really deep stuff. Anybody can talk about that leash stuff and the circle of opportunity and blah-blah-blah. Now, I go the extra mile. I'm about to be vulnerable.

You know what I thought as I was sitting there watching my dog gnaw my leg off. *Yeah, but at least I don't drool. And I don't chase my tail. If I had one I might, but I don't.*

That's right, I compared myself to our dog, and sadly, I felt really good about it. He looks for a treat every time he comes in the house and goes to his kennel. That's a big deal to him. How utterly pathetic! I don't do that.

Then I looked at his leg and wondered how it would feel to gnaw it, just a little, but then my kids came home and took him for a walk.

On good days, it doesn't feel like I'm on a leash. On bad days you'll find me straining and wearing a groove in the grass as I look in the next yard. My prayer is that I'll recognize all the good things my Owner has given today. I want to be happy just to see him. I want to long for his presence.

When that happens, maybe I'll know what it's like to have a tail.

Chippie Doesn't Sing Much Anymore

Marvin Phillips

A Texas newspaper reported the story. A Galveston housewife had a pet parakeet named Chippie. The woman made several mistakes. She was vacuuming her floors, and she decided to clean out the bottom of Chippie's cage with her vacuum cleaner. Mistake number one.

The phone rang. She turned to answer the phone without turning off the machine. You guessed it. Sssssssp! Chippie got sucked through the tube and into the canister. Mistake number two.

She dropped the phone, shut off the vacuum cleaner, and opened up the canister. There was Chippie—feathers askew, dirt all over his little body, stunned but alive. She rushed into the bathroom, bird in hand. She held Chippie under the faucet and turned it on full blast. Mistake number three.

Then she spotted the hair dryer. She turned it to "Hot" and "High." Mistake number four. The blast did the trick, but it nearly finished Chippie.

The next day the reporter called to check on the bird. "How's your poor parakeet?" the reporter inquired. It was about the reply you'd expect: "Well, Chippie doesn't sing much anymore. He just sort of sits there and stares."

I have the feeling many of you can relate to Chippie. You've had your cage vacuumed. You've felt sucked into the dirt bag, stuck under the faucet, and hit with a blast from a hair blower. And you don't sing much anymore. You just sort of sit there and stare.

I believe we were born to sing. Hank Williams sings the line, "I was born to boogie." I believe it's in the nature of all of us to be singers. Positive thinkers. Lots of people believe they were born naked. I believe you were born with a bright red ribbon wrapped around your body. On that ribbon were the words, "I am Lovable and Capable."

There are lots of Chippie-style circumstances that steal our songs. Life sucks us all into the tube. People pour cold water on our dreams. Disappointment and disaster blow us away. Many people believe in Murphy's Law: What *can* go wrong *will* go wrong. Others believe in O'Toole's law: "Murphy was an optimist!"

Somewhere in the trauma of things, like Chippie, many people lose their songs. They just sort of sit there and stare.

Some people choose to be croakers. Whiners. Complainers. Someone said, "Don't tell other people your problems. Eighty percent don't care, and the other 20 percent are kind of glad it happened to you." I don't know about that, but I do know we can all choose our attitudes.

Our world is full of cage vacuumers, hair blowers, and song stealers. It's nice to know you don't have to just sit there and stare.

Open your mouth and sing this song by L. B. Bridges at the top of your voice,

> "Jesus, Jesus, Jesus,
> Sweetest name I know,
> Fills my every longing,
> Keeps me singing as I go."

Pet Peeves

Chris Ewing

Pets can be a wonderful experience for your children. They can teach many lessons about life—responsibility, friendship, pain. They are a part of growing up and a part of learning about this wonderfully diverse world in which we live. Unfortunately, as a father, you must also be prepared for the downside of pet ownership. Here are a few of the possibilities you may (or may not) want to investigate.

Aquaticus Toileticus (Fish)

What can I say about goldfish? We tried them. Of course, we've tried everything. The kids said, in unison, "Dad, we want fish. All our friends have fish. Why can't we have fish?" No rehearsing here, nosiree.

"Fish sticks or fillets?" I asked. "Salmon or flounder?"

"Live fish, Dad. That swim in a tank."

Oh. That kind of fish.

"We have a cat. Cats eat fish. Besides," I added, "fish stink. They are cold and wet and they stink. And you can't cuddle up to them like a small, furry animal."

The kids brightened up.

"Can we have a hamster? We could get a boy hamster and a girl hamster and they could have babies and we could sell them and make lots of money! Pleeeese?"

"Let me see if that old fish tank is still in the garage attic."

Chewitus Upitus (Small Furry Mammals)

You cannot have a cat and small, furry animals in the house at the same time. This just does not work. Of course, the children do not understand this concept and eventually you are dragged screaming and kicking from the house by the entire family and told you will not be allowed to return without a small, furry animal in tow. So we loaded up the car and headed off into the sunset to look for some obnoxious little rodent. I would have been glad to set a trap in the garden, but, no, that wasn't quite what they were looking for.

Luckily, the local discount store carried small, furry animals at a reduced price. Their habitat, however, came at a premium. I decided a shoe box would be sufficient. Who needs a high-rise plastic-and-metal condominium for a rat, anyway? Not to mention food, water bottles, bedding, chew toys, vitamins, etcetera.

So we went home and everyone agreed that the little hamster is cute and we built a nice little house for it and the kids went to sleep with smiles of contentment on their cherubic faces.

I would have been glad to set a trap in the garden, but, no, that wasn't quite what they were looking for.

The next morning the cat was not hungry and the shoe box was empty and I found a cute little rodent foot under the kitchen table.

"Anyone want an unlucky rodent foot?" No takers.

We went back to the discount store and got another little mammal and a high-rise plastic-and-steel condominium. I had to admit, this worked ever so much better than a shoe box. It was fun, at least for a while, to watch the little creature run through convoluted tunnels that never went anywhere and jog on his little hamster treadmill that had a squeak that could be heard throughout the house at two in the morning.

However, a warning about small, furry animals. They are escape artists and they are very curious. They will squeeze or eat their way through any opening just so they can get a closer look at, for instance, a cat. Little do they realize it will be their last look at a mammal higher up on the food chain than they are. These little rodents have been known to chew holes through doors to sacrifice themselves in this manner. We decided they must be part lemming or something and no longer feed our feline in this manner.

Felinus Aloofnus (Cats)

As any cat owner will attest, felines are a different kind of animal. They have always suited me as they require a minimum of attention and man and beast can generally just ignore each other. A few years back, however, we had a visitor that couldn't be ignored.

Late one night, I heard all kinds of strange sounds coming from our basement. Bumps. Thumps. I got out of bed and went down to investigate. I flipped on the light to the stairs to hear an immediate crash as something glass shattered. I grabbed the baseball bat behind the door and crept silently downward.

Someone, or some thing, was in the process of trashing the basement, which wasn't hard to do since it was used only for storage. Boxes lay scattered on the floor. The remains of a glass lamp lay in the corner. I crept onward and noticed an outside window was open a crack. Suddenly, like in a B horror movie, this blob of fur sprang out from behind the washing machine and went tearing across the floor.

A cat. Some unfortunate had gotten in through the window and couldn't get out. Well, I'd better help him out before my kids saw the mangy creature and wanted to adopt it.

I advanced slowly toward the animal and noticed he didn't look too well. Some of us lead rougher lives than others, I guess.

"Here, kitty, kitty," I said soothingly. "Let me help you out."

I put the bat down so I could pick up the cat with both hands. With a yowl that made me jump, the cat suddenly attacked. I threw up my left hand to shield my face and throat. The cat grabbed onto the right. I stepped backward, tripped on the bat, and went down. Now the wild beast had the upper hand, so to speak, and pressed on with the attack, chewing like mad. I jumped up, screaming bloody murder, and finally managed to frantically shake the leech off my hand. He ran off into a corner, eyeing me and spitting and hissing. I ran off into the opposite corner, eyeing him and spitting and hissing and calculating the chances that I could reach the bat on the floor between us. It was a standoff.

Suddenly, like in a B horror movie, this blob of fur sprang out from behind the washing machine and went tearing across the floor.

My wife appeared at the top of the stairs.

"Do not come down!" I yelled. "There is a deranged monster down here! Shut the door and lock it behind you!"

"Really," she sleepily muttered as she shut the door. "You flatter yourself too much."

Click went the lock.

Now I was locked in with this creature. I wasn't in any mood for another encounter of the bloody kind, so I eased around to the basement door, the cat turning and spitting at me every foot of the way. I opened the outside door wide and backed off. It took awhile and I had to throw a number of boxes and articles of clothing at it before it finally got the idea and made a dash for freedom.

The doctor was very understanding as she administered a tetanus shot and sewed up my hand.

"And where is this creature now?" she asked.

"In some other state, I hope," I replied.

She thought a minute before continuing. "I'd like to discuss something with you, something that is fairly common around here—and extremely unpleasant."

I looked up at the sudden change in her voice.

"Let's talk rabies."

"I'll find the cat," I replied.

The neighbors thought I was nuts, creeping around the bushes at all hours of the day and night and meowing like a cat in heat. I left little cans of open cat food around the back door. I warned the children not to go outside or the "bogey-cat" would eat them. But my time was running out.

One sleepless night after dreaming dark dreams of werewolves,

I checked the "catch-them-alive" trap at the back door. Bingo. One spitting, hissing ball of fury. He lived in the garage, well caged and well fed, until his (and my) ten-day sentence was up and then went to live with friends in the country.

The kids still get a kick out of my reenactment of the whole fight scene. I take a stuffed toy cat and hold it up to my neck with both hands and struggle and gurgle with my eyes rolled back in their sockets. Then I tear it from my throat and fling it against the wall and beat on it with a pillow.

"And that's how it was," I pant. The kids love it.

Caninus Pesti-plenti-cuss (Dogs)

If you are a normal father, sooner or later you are going to consider getting a cute, adorable little puppy for a child of yours. The child will beg you and bother you and draw doggie pictures and sing doggie songs and promise to take care of it until you succumb to the constant, insidious brainwashing.

Don't give in.

Just say "no."

If you want that kind of pain, just go out to the garage, find a two-by-four, and start beating yourself on the head with it. It hurts just the same and is a lot less expensive. I know. Really. You see, I was brainwashed once.

I still don't know how it happened but, the first thing I knew, my wife and I were driving around town looking at dogs. We finally decided a puppy was in order and ended up getting a hound. The pup's mother was so calm and nice we

Little did we know that the pup's father was a carrier of the dreaded Caninus Desperadus, a.k.a. the "Doggy Desperado" gene.

knew this was the dog for us. Little did we know that the pup's father was a carrier of the dreaded Caninus Desperadus, a.k.a. the "doggy desperado" gene. We suspected this much after the dog grew. He had a strong voice—a hound voice, low but powerful, something akin to an old-fashioned train whistle. Carried for miles. Just ask anyone in the neighborhood. He also got big fast, bigger than his mom. And strong! This animal could yank me right off my feet and had no problem whatsoever in pulling the kids through cactus and rocks.

Now, this worried me somewhat, especially after the time Dog ran into Daughter headfirst during some especially rambunctious play. The thunk these two hard heads made coming together echoed all over the backyard. I ran over to help my daughter off the ground and was shocked by the true goose-egg bruise on her forehead and the glazed look in her eyes.

"How many fingers?" I asked as I held four of my digits up in front of her.

"How many who?" she asked.

"Fingers. On my hand."

She struggled in vain to focus.

"Eighteen? Say, who are you, anyway?"

From that time on, no one was allowed to be on the same level as Dog. This wasn't easy to enforce since he could also jump up and put his paws on my shoulders and, if he stood on tip-paws, look me square in the face with those big, mournful brown eyes. Who could resist?

But the love-hate relationship with this animal took an abrupt lean toward the latter when we went on a short trip and had a friend come over to feed, water, and play with our half-grown pup—who was living outside full time.

Our minivacation didn't go so well. It was one of those vacations where you wish you would have just gone and burned your money because it would have been more fun and less exhausting, if you know what I mean. I was really looking forward to getting back home so I could relax. But when we arrived home and I opened up the front door, who should greet us but Mr. Break-and-Enter Mutt.

"Uh-oh," I said.

I looked around the house.

"Oh. My."

I dropped the suitcases. My wife dropped hers. The kids dropped theirs. The dog continued to race up and down the stairs, barking incessantly and showing off what was left of all the great things he had discovered.

As far as we could piece together, this is what happened: After our friend had fed, watered, and played with the Destroyer and gone home, the dog had apparently pried the outside screen off one of the basement windows. He then proceeded to somehow open both the storm window and the inside window. He jumped into the house, knocking over and breaking a lamp. He ate the cat food. He drank from toilets. He scattered as much garbage as possible around the house. He ate the kids' stuffed animals. He ate the kids' plastic toys. Like Goldilocks, he tried everyone's chair and bed. He had to go to the bathroom. Any number of times. He opened the kitchen cupboards and ate my son's Koco-Krunchies and anything else he could find. He got sick. Several times.

What could I do?

I calmly put Destructo out in the backyard (what yard?)

where he belonged, went out in the garage, and started beating myself on the head with a two-by-four.

It took a full day, a rented carpet shampooer, and a trip to the landfill before I could get the house close to its original condition. But it never has been quite the same.

Above all, I have tried to instill in my children an attitude of respect and love for all living creatures. Every creature, from the lowly earthworm to the majestic whale, has its place on this fragile planet and in God's universe according to His divine plan. We, as stewards of these gifts, dare not abuse the trust that has been placed in us to humanely care for and use these creatures and the earthly environment we all share. As the hymn teaches us, "All things bright and beautiful, all creatures great and small, all things wise and wonderful, the Lord God made them all."

Princess Fur-Face

Marilyn Meberg

"Whad'ya say we change the furniture around?" Ken queried one Saturday morning as we were finishing our last cups of coffee/tea. "Let's put the couch by the window and the two chairs facing the fireplace." I had learned years before to trust Ken's fine eye for furniture placement.

"Sounds good to me, Babe," I said, "but do you have the stamina for Ashley's neurotic response?"

Ashley was our cocker spaniel who reacted strongly against all visual changes. She wanted things to remain in their accustomed spots. If they didn't, she had one of her "spells." It didn't matter how big or small the change; each warranted a protest. Let me give you an example.

A friend popped in on me one morning and for some reason just dropped her purse in the middle of the floor as we made our way to the "chat chairs" by the window. (This was before the rearrangement.) Several moments later Ashley, who hated to miss anything, came trotting into the room. Spotting my friend's purse in the middle of the floor, she skidded to a stiff-legged halt, stared briefly at the purse, and went into a dramatic fit of barking. Slowly circling the purse, she barked, growled, and scowled until my friend finally placed her purse behind the chair. Gradually Ashley settled down, but it was obvious the visit was ruined for her.

As Ken pondered the price to be paid for furniture rearrangement, he noted that Ashley was out on the deck dozing in the sun. She might not notice what was going on until the dastardly deed was done.

Several hours later Ashley roused herself from her siesta and ambled into the house. She immediately assessed that unauthorized changes had occurred in her absence. After barking herself nearly hoarse, she flounced out of the living room and stayed in her "sleep area" for several days. We delivered her food and water. Gradually she came to realize that the couch was now in a far better spot for her because she was able to see out the window. (Of course she was allowed on the furniture!) This made it possible for her to visually patrol the neighborhood without leaving the comforts of home.

Perhaps the greatest trauma Princess Fur-Face had to endure was when we got a new car. Ashley's sleep area was in a small room adjoining the garage, and although the car wasn't fully visible to her, it was in close proximity.

On the first night of their cohabitation, Ashley, who had not yet been introduced to the new car, scampered down the stairs to bed as was her custom. We stood behind the closed door holding our breath. No sound…no barking…no response at all. Ken's theory was that because it was dark, Ashley couldn't see the car. Our intention was to later, in the daylight, gradually coax her into an accepting relationship with the new vehicle.

Around 1 A.M. we were awakened by the sound of frantic, ferocious barking. Ashley had discovered the car. Fearing she'd disturb the neighbors, Ken flew down the stairs, scooped up Ashley along with her bed, and deposited her in our room, something Ken normally refused to do. She grumbled and complained the rest of the night, but at least she didn't bark.

Because Ken drove the car to work during the day, I had no opportunity to ease Ashley into a spirit of charitableness about the car. Each night she seemed to forget about the alien in the garage when she first went to bed, then rediscover it sometime after midnight.

At 2 A.M. on the fourth night of Ashley's histrionics, Ken exasperatedly dragged himself out of bed and announced he had just come up with a plan which required that we both get dressed and take Ashley for a ride.

"Are you going to dump her out of the car somewhere in another county?" I asked cautiously as I threw on jeans and a sweatshirt.

"Trust me" was all he said.

Ken thrust a squirming, growling, barking cocker into my arms, and we got in the monster car to begin what Ken said would be the "taming ride." For at least an hour Ashley was a bundle of growling rigidity in my arms. With the radio playing soft music and both of us stroking Ashley with words of love and encouragement (none of which we felt at that moment), Ashley began to relax. An hour and a half later and miles from home, she went limp in my arms and fell asleep. From that moment on,

Ashley had peace about her metal roommate. In fact, one of her favorite activities became riding in that car.

I hate to tell you how closely I identify with Ashley at times. There are God-gifts I have fought so fervently only to find that once I yield my resisting spirit I reap incredible benefits. For example, I certainly don't overly resist the concept of grace, but I've tried to earn it a million times. I seem to tenaciously cling to the mistaken notion that I've got to be good enough in order to deserve grace. How many times does God have to hold my rigidly resisting spirit until finally, with celestial music in my ears, I relax and embrace his gift?

Ashley learned with just one ride.

Chapter 11

love and laughter—

humoR in marriage

That's Matrimony

If you do housework for $150 a week, that's domestic service. If you do it for nothing— that's matrimony.

—FROM IS YOUR LOVE TANK FULL?,
DENNIS SWANBERG

Adam and Eve

John William Smith

"And the LORD God fashioned into a woman the rib which
He had taken from the man, and brought her to the man."

—Genesis 2:22

"I have something for you, Adam."

"*Wow!*" (his response translated roughly). "Where did you
find that—it—I mean—*Wow!* I thought I'd already seen and
named everything you'd made."

"I didn't *find* her, Adam; I *made* her. I made her for you."

"Is that what you were doing while I was asleep? Did you say
her?"

"Yes, *her.*"

"You mean, she's like me—except she's the *other kind?*"

"Yes."

"Thank you very much! She's…well, she's *great*, I mean she's
perfect."

The Maker left them to themselves. And although He knew what would happen, it gave him real pleasure to watch it for the first time—*the way of a man with a maid.* It began, as it has always begun—with talk.

"The Maker called you *Adam?*"

"Yes, that's my name."

"Am I to have a name?"

"Well, I suppose so. I've named everything else. Let's see, I've got it. *Eve!* That's it; I'll call you *Eve.* How do you like that?"

"It's not very creative—I think I like Adam better. Why can't I be Adam?"

"Well, that would be stupid. It wouldn't make sense if we both had the same name—besides, names mean things, and you *can't* be Adam because Adam means man and you aren't man—you're—boy, are you good looking! I seem to have lost my train of thought. What was I saying?"

"You were saying something about the meaning of my name and why it couldn't be Adam. What is 'boy,' and what is 'train of thought'?"

"Oh yes, well, what I was saying is that you are woman, because you came out of me. You see, God, the Maker, took one of my ribs—look; see the scar? *Don't touch it!* Good grief, it's still sore—anyway—he formed you out of my rib, and that's why I named you Eve, because that's what your name means; and 'boy' is another word for man—except it means young man; and 'train of thought' is a saying that will come into existence about ten thousand years from now when there are things called 'trains'—and please don't ask me to explain that, but it means to pursue a systematic pattern of thought."

"Oh. Seems silly to me. What are you so excited about, any-

way? I just thought I liked the name Adam. Are your answers to questions always so long and complicated? I really don't care what you call me. And if 'boy' means young man, why did you call me that? I thought you said I wasn't man, and what does 'good grief' and 'make sense' mean?"

"'Make sense' is like *logical,* like one thing follows another, like if this is true then that is true; and 'boy' is used—oh forget it; and 'good grief' is a colloquialism, and don't you dare ask me what that means; and if you didn't care, then why make such a fuss? I've named sixteen zillion things—took me about a thousand days! You never saw such a line up of animals, and I named 'em—every last one I named! Thought sure I'd run out of words, but I named them all—from terns, tigers, and tyrannosauruses to parakeets, petrels, and penguins—man, I thought He had me on penguins—did you ever see a penguin? Funniest thing He ever made except camels, platypuses, and kangaroos. Now those kangaroos—"

"Adam, I think you lost your 'train of thought' again."

"What? Oh yes, what I was saying was—let me tell you, if you were *me* standing here looking at *you,* you'd lose your train of thought too."

"You were going to make some point about my making a fuss over my name."

"Well, yes, I was. I was going to say that I had named fourteen zillion things—"

"You said sixteen zillion last time."

"There you go again—see—fourteen zillion, sixteen zillion. It's just a figure of speech—"

"A what?"

"A figure of speech, you know, a figure of—man, speaking

"If you were me standing here looking at you, you'd lose your train of thought too.

of figures—you've got one; I mean, you're *beautiful.* I've never seen anything quite like you—and I've seen a lot. Did you ever see an elephant or a hippopotamus? Man, they're something! And right when I was naming the hippopotamus—I only had 'hippo' out—two male leopards got into it over some female leopard, and I thought we were going to have a riot until another female leopard showed up and—"

"Adam, you were going to tell me about a figure of speech."

"Well, yes, I was, except I keep losing track of where I am and you keep interrupting. I've named twenty-five zil— fourteen zil—a whole gob of animals—and not one single one ever argued about their name. They just said, 'Yes sir; thank you sir,' and they went right on."

"But I'm not an animal. Does a figure of speech *make sense?*"

"Yes, of course, and boy, you're sure not an animal—and you ask the darndest questions—and am I ever glad—that you're not an animal, I mean. You know, you're sensational; I mean, *you're a ten.* I don't know how He did it."

"Did what? And what's a ten?"

"Made something like you, and a ten is another figure of speech that means perfect. I mean, He's made some pretty fantastic stuff, but you are the greatest!"

"You're not half bad yourself, Adam. In fact, you're by far the most attractive thing I've seen since I got here."

"You mean it? You really think I'm good looking? Have you seen the orangutans and the giraffes? Speaking of giraffes, the other day two of them got into the garden, and it infuriated me—I mean—they've got the whole world to eat in, and they got into *my* garden. I chased them about ten miles before I—"

"You're not half bad yourself, Adam."

"What's a mile? And what is a garden?"

"Well, a mile is a long way. It's from here to—well, about to that live oak over there by the river—and the garden, well, that's where we live."

"We?"

"Well, sure, you and I—I mean, that is if you want to. I don't mean to be pushy, but I sure would like for you to live with me—it would be great! And now that I've seen you, I think the Maker meant for us to live together; it wouldn't seem right not to, because—well, you know—the giraffes live together and the eagles—man, you can't separate them. In fact, it was only about three weeks ago one of them hurt its wing, and the other one wouldn't leave it for anything—brought it food and protected it and—"

"Adam."

"Yes."

"Adam, I would love to live with you in your garden or any other place you wish. There are many things I don't know, but I do know that *my place is with you,* and it always will be."

"You would? I mean, it is? Wow! And to think you chose me."

"Adam, what is 'chose'?"

And so it always was, and so it will ever be, the greatest of all God's miracles—that two things, when seen standing apart, appear so incorrigibly different and diametrically opposed but when placed together fit so wonderfully well. No one understands it, and the more we study it and try to "make sense" of it and force the two to be the same, the more trouble we have making it work. Perhaps it wasn't meant to be figured out—only to be wondered at and appreciated.

Shut the D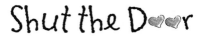r
Laura Jensen Walker

All my life I've been a sucker for romance. I blubber like a baby whenever I see *West Side Story*. Especially the tragic ending when Maria cradles the dead Tony's head in her lap and lovingly whispers, *"Te adoro,* Anton," as the tears run down her face.

There goes half a box of Kleenex every time.

Another one of my favorite romantic movies is *The Parent Trap.* I thought it was so romantic the way the double Hayley Mills's parents in the movie (the sexy, rugged Brian Keith and the beautiful and sophisticated Maureen O'Hara) finally got back together after being divorced for so many years.

But for all that romance, there was one thing about the movie that always used to bug me. Near the end, when the mom and dad are eating dinner, Brian realizes he's still in love with ex-wife Maureen and starts to tell her. However, right in the middle of his incredibly romantic and endearing speech, she points out that he's gotten some stew on himself. He tells her he doesn't care, but she can't concentrate on what he's saying. All she focuses on is the stew. And she tells him to go and wash it off!

"What's the matter with you, woman?" I used to scream at the TV screen. "Don't you have any romance in your soul? This is a big romantic moment. Let this wonderful, sexy man sweep you off your feet."

Then I got married.

Many women have to contend with husbands who don't put the toilet seat down. I'm lucky. I don't have that problem because Michael grew up in a household with four women, so he was well-trained by the time I got him (although there was one time early in our marriage when I got up in the middle of the night to go to the bathroom and fell into the black hole of Calcutta).

(It never happened again.)

I wish I could say the same for his shut-the-door handicap.

Without fail, every day when Michael gets ready for work, he never shuts his dresser drawers all the way. Sure, he pushes them in after he pulls out his socks and underwear, but never all the way. I don't get it. Just another inch or two and they'd be shut. How hard is that?

But by far the most difficult thing for me is an open closet door in the bedroom. When I'm lying in bed reading, I simply can't concentrate on my book when out of the corner of my eye I see a mishmash of shirts and pants, a hodge-podge of sweaters tossed every which way, Mickey Mouse suspenders peeping from inside a tux, and a jumble of shoes on the floor.

I like—no, need—to see order and beauty around me. And an open closet door is simply jarring to my senses. So I usually get up and close it.

I discovered I can't concentrate on other things, either, when the closet door is open. One night, when Michael was in a particularly romantic mood, he began kissing my neck. Things were just beginning to heat up when over his shoulder I suddenly noticed the open closet door. "Just a minute," I said, leaping out of bed in a single bound to shut it.

"Way to wreck a mood," Michael said wryly.

A few days later, it was my turn to be in an amorous state of mind. So I put on some Sinatra, lit the beeswax candles, and donned one of my Victoria's Secret bridal shower gifts. Then I led my adorable husband into our bedroom where I began gently nuzzling his neck and whispering sweet nothings in his ear.

Remembering Natalie Wood's endearment in *West Side Story*, yet recalling that she had said it to the dead Tony, I chose a French translation instead. *"Je t'adore"* (pronounced "zhuhtuh-door"), I murmured to Michael in my huskiest bedroom voice.

"Shut the door?" he asked in some confusion, glancing at the closet door. "The door is shut."

To this day, "Shut the Door" in our house means "I Love You."

How to Handle a Woman
Becky Freeman

Men should know that women sometimes get together and play a game called "Let's Compare Husbands." It's a lot like a card game, actually. And, as with face cards, not all hubby's personality traits have equal value. According to the rule book, having the correct combinations is also important. I've played a few rounds myself and have had some pretty stiff competition, but usually I'm assured of having at least one ace in the hole. This is the way it goes.

"All right, girls," Player Number One says, "I'm holding a man who picks up his own socks and knows how to whip up a box of macaroni and cheese by himself."

"Wow," replies Player Number Two. "That's hard to beat. But I'll raise you. My husband can unstop a backed-up commode and doesn't mind changing the cat box."

"Oh, you're kidding!" says Player Number Three. "You've got

a man with a strong stomach? All I've got is a regular paycheck coming in, a great father to the kids, and no snoring at night."

"Well, ladies," I say as I lay down my cards with a flourish. "Read 'em and weep. I've got a husband who's stubborn, knows how to say just the wrong thing at just the wrong time, and has the patience of a gnat. But when he's good, he's very, very good. He's tender. He's playful. And girls, I'm sorry to have to tell you this, but—he's also romantic."

"Oh, pooh!" the rest lament. "It's not fair—Becky's holding the King of Hearts again!"

I may be slightly overstating the case, but I haven't yet met a woman who wouldn't trade neatness and steadiness for a man who enjoys candlelight dinners, interesting conversations, and is known to, on occasion, waltz his wife across the kitchen floor.

I know there are many men out there who think romantic equals softness equals big sissy. Most of these men, unfortunately, are dateless, divorced, or sleeping on the couch. Take it from me—the surest way to a woman's heart is the most direct route. Go straight for the heart.

When I think of romance and tenderness in our relationship, I think of the countless little things that add to our love. The way our bodies "spoon" together when we snuggle close at night. The way we sometimes talk to each other like little kids just because it's fun. When Scott completes a special project on the house, he may come grab my hand and in a boyish voice urge, "Come see my big roof!"...

I love the way Scott graciously reads my work while allowing me to stare at him, taking note of every twitch, every minuscule response. By some miracle, he's able to completely tune out the fact that my face is five inches away from his. He just pencils his critique as if I'm invisible. Then he always tells me the truth—where the manuscript made him laugh, where it touched him, where he had no idea what on earth I was trying to say. Once the writing project is a wrap, I can always count on one thing: He will be prouder of me than any other human being on the face of the earth.

But most of all, I've enjoyed the slow dances to old love songs pouring from the kitchen radio.

I like this man. Very much.

Madeleine L'Engle penned the tender love story of her marriage to Hugh Franklin in the book, *Two-Part Invention: The Story of a Marriage.* Near the end of the story, there's a heartbreaking scene where Madeleine is holding her husband in her arms as he takes his last breath. She was unable, for several moments, to release her embrace. At one point, she turned to the attending physician and said, "It is hard to let go beloved flesh." Madeleine finished the book with a beautiful line from a poem by Conrad Aiken, a poem Hugh had read to her some forty years earlier on the night he proposed marriage:

Music I heard with you was more than music,
And bread I broke with you was more than bread.

I cannot read those words without thinking of Scott, and I cannot think long on them without tears coming to my eyes. For one day I, too, may have to "let go beloved flesh." And when I do, it will be my husband's tender, romantic expressions that I'll surely miss the most. No, moments like that don't happen all the time, but when they do, they make even everyday "bread and music" extraordinary.

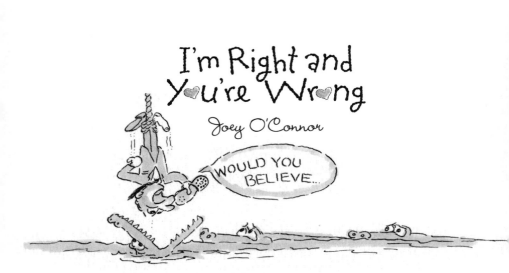

I'm Right and You're Wrong

Joey O'Connor

WOULD YOU BELIEVE...

I can remember getting home from school when I was a kid, raiding the refrigerator, and lying down on our lime-green shag carpet to watch one of my favorite television shows, *Get Smart*. I loved laughing at the Chief, Larabee, Hymie the CONTROL robot, Siegfried, Schtarker, Admiral Hargrade, and, of course, the ever self-confident, but completely clumsy Secret Agent Maxwell Smart. I also had a crush on Agent 99, but what guy didn't? I always wished we had a telephone booth with a secret elevator in our house. What I really needed was the "Cone of Silence" so my parents couldn't hear my friends and me sharing our fifth-grade secrets. Never could find a pair of those telephone shoes.

Whenever Maxwell Smart was surrounded by KAOS agents or hanging upside down over a pool of hungry alligators, what did he always do to get out of his predicament? He went to extremes.

In his sharp, shrill voice, Maxwell Smart resorted to blustery warnings of cataclysmic harm if anyone laid a finger on him. Who could forget such classic Maxwell Smart lines as these:

- At this very minute, twenty-five CONTROL agents are converging on this building. Would you believe two squad cars and a motorcycle cop? How about a vicious street cleaner and a toothless police dog?

- As soon as you're gone, by the use of sheer brute strength I shall be able to rip these chains from the wall in one minute. Would you believe it? One minute. Would you believe two minutes? How about a week from Tuesday?

- You better drop that gun because this yacht happens to be surrounded by the Seventh Fleet. Would you believe the Sixth Fleet? How about a school of angry flounder?

- In a short while, General Crawford and a hundred of his crack paratroopers will come crashing into this landing. Would you believe J. Edgar Hoover and ten of his G-men? How about Tarzan and a couple of apes? Bomba the jungle Boy?

Because Maxwell Smart was desperate to escape the evil clutches of KAOS agents, he naturally went to extremes. Daily, he and Agent 99 battled KAOS agents who were pursuing world domination. Though Max was a CONTROL agent, we all know that his life and the perplexing pickles he found himself in were anything but controlled. He had to single-handedly outwit KAOS agents who tried to outsmart him with dastardly deeds like:

- The old bulletproof-cummerbund-in-the-tuxedo trick.

- The old remote-control-self-propelled-spinning-door-knob trick.

- The old drug-his-prunes, fake-the-fight, ransack-the-apartment, and switch-places-with-the-Admiral trick.

- The old Professor-Peter-Peckinpah-all-purpose-anti-personnel-pocket-pistol-under-the-toupee trick.

When you and your spouse square off and say to each other in one way or another, "I'm right and you're wrong," what you've got going on is a battle between KAOS and CONTROL. It's the old you-won't-win-this-one-no-matter-how-hard-you-pout-scream-whine-huff-slam-the-door-I'm-not-sleeping-on-the-couch-*YOU-SLEEP-ON-THE-COUCH*-what-in-the-world-was-I-thinking-when-I-married-you-somebody-must've-slipped-me-a-mickey trick. Each spouse is claiming that they're on the CONTROL team.

I'm Maxwell Smart.

No, I'm Agent 99.

Nobody wants to be the bad guy.

Nobody wants to be Siegfried, the leader of KAOS.

One of the first things Krista and I learned in our premarital counseling class was that we were to remove two extreme words from our soon-to-be marriage vocabulary: *always* and *never*. We were clearly told never to say "always" and never to say "never."

Ever.

What was that counselor smoking? *Always* and *never* are the twin silver bullets of every good argument. *Always* and *never* are the North and South Poles for every point, principle, or position on the compass of marital communication.

Always and never are the twin silver bullets of every good argument.

They are the moral high ground for winning your way in marriage. There is no more effective way to put your spouse on the defensive than staking your claim on either side of *always* and *never*. What better way to make your point than by using such precise, authoritative, righteous, and wieldy-sounding words: *You always do this—you never do that.*

Always is the best offense and *never* is the best defense.

Always and *never* are the Malta of the Marriage Mediterranean.

Control these two words and you control the world!

Scientists have confirmed that marriage is the most extreme relationship among all living things. Except perhaps for the black widow and her soon-to-be-eaten mate, marriage is the epitome of extremes in God's wild kingdom. Put a man and woman together for a few years, throw in a couple of kids, some pets, a mortgage, conflicting schedules, job stress, a stack of bills thicker than the wad in your wallet, and the natural order is chaos. Marriage is anything but control.

As a CONTROL agent, Maxwell Smart understood this important scientific principle, and so he threw caution to the wind and flew by the seat of his pants. In the midst of chaos, he was unflappable. Unstoppable. Brazenly bold. Supremely confident. And why?

Max knew he couldn't control all the chaos, but the one thing he could control was himself.

Maybe Max and Agent 99 have something to teach us all about marriage. Life is a constant, changing state of chaos and control. And marriage may be an accurate reflection of this broken world that causes aliens looking at us from outer space to scratch their antennae and wonder, "What on earth are these people doing?"

The illusion of control we strive for in marriage is as elusive as getting help from an HMO customer service representative. There is never one part of any marriage that is completely under control. Just when you think you've got your finances under control, the transmission goes out on your car. Just when you think you've raised the perfect kid, the vice principal is on the phone. Just when you think you're a romantic Don Juan, your wife calls you Señor Postmortem.

The heart of most spousal skirmishes is the need to be in control. When one spouse feels threatened by the other, it's easy to go to extremes. When no one wants to back down and admit when they're truly wrong, then what you have is chaos.

Getting on common ground is work, and building a marriage that is constantly changing amid the chaos of life is hard work. It means being willing to look at problems, conflicts, and situations from our spouse's perspective. It means giving up our need for control. It means admitting that there is more chaos in our life than we'd like to admit, that we don't have it all together.

If you've recently gone to extremes with your spouse and pulled a marital red card, go ahead and wave the white flag. Say you're sorry. Forgive as God has forgiven you. Ask God for peace in the midst of the chaos. Get on common ground. Talk about your differences and celebrate the fact that your spouse is not your clone. If that were the case, you'd really have chaos.

Appreciate the unique differences in your spouse instead of allowing those differences to divide you. Control yourself, not your spouse. Do this and you'll get smart.

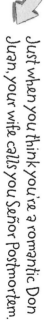

Just when you think you're a romantic Don Juan, your wife calls you Señor Postmortem.

Chapter 12

the funny thing
about
grace

A Daily Prayer

I want to thank you, Lord, for being close to me so far this day. With your help I haven't been impatient, lost my temper, been grumpy, judgmental, or envious of anyone. But I will be getting out of bed in a minute, and I think I will really need your help then. Amen.

—FROM HOLY HILARITY, CAL AND ROSE SAMRA

Wiped Out

Patsy Clairmont

"Mom, Mom, come quick! You've got to see what's on TV," Jason insisted.

Certain it would be something to make housework easier, I raced to the living room. Much to my surprise, the young girl on the screen leaned forward and announced, "I've got a zit right here," pointing to her nose. "But it's okay," she encouraged, "because I have a stick of Erase."

Confused (and unamused) I stared at Jason, who sheepishly confessed, "Well, I just thought maybe you could use it on those...those...wrinkles." He gestured toward my well-deserved grooves of maturity.

"These are not wrinkles," I stated clearly.

Jason surveyed my face again, as if he was reading a well-worn map. "They look just like wrin—" he stammered, losing confidence as I moved toward him.

"Jason," I interrupted, "this is depth! The good Lord has just entrusted some of us with more depth than others."

I marched off, feeling insulted or at least slightly defaced. I thought about the girl on TV and remembered her remedy. I began to picture a stick of Erase, in fact a great big stick. Then I mentally erased Jason.

That was such fun I began to think of others who had said or done something I didn't appreciate. I thought of our eldest son, Marty.

Each day I would meet him at the door with a melodic greeting as he returned from work. His typical response was to grunt. I erased him.

Then my husband came to mind. Now he never actually says it, but at times his attitude seems to shout, "Is this all you've done today?" Erase.

I was really getting into this game. I thought of other family members, neighbors, checkout clerks, co-workers, bank tellers, beauticians…

Now, the only drawback to this mental game was that everyone at one time or another had said or done something I didn't appreciate. By the time I erased them, it left me all alone. Somehow I didn't like the company.

I began to think of some things I've said or done I wished I could erase—like the last hasty word I felt "led" to say, or my unloving attitude with the clerk who was too slow, or the years I lost to agoraphobia, house-bound in fear. This game wasn't much fun after all.

Then I remembered that God provided a stick of Erase—a permanent eraser, the shed blood of Jesus. Our sins and iniquities He remembers no more—erase!

What a relief. What a release.

G♥d's E-mail

Barbara Johnson

A little girl was learning the Lord's Prayer. Each night at bedtime her mother carefully repeated it. At last the child was ready to try it on her own. She knelt down, folded her hands, and began to pray. Each line was perfect until: "...and lead us not into temptation...but deliver us some e-mail."

God chuckles at our innocent mistakes. And he proclaims truth through children, because God does deliver e-mail—just when we need it most! The King of kings gives you and me access into his grace over the phone line of faith—direct to his royal chat room. His e-mail address is Jeremiah33:3@don'tstress.com: "Call to me and I will answer you and tell you great and unsearchable things you do not know."

Some of us are technologically challenged. I understand that. It can be intimidating to get into a brand new mode of communication when you're used to old-fashioned tools like telephones, typewriters, or even fountain pens. Once I sat down at a computer [and]…put my disk into the slot. Nothing appeared on the screen, so I called Computerland for help. The service department told me to put my disk back into the slot and be sure to close the door. I told the customer service guy to hold on. When I got up and closed the door to my office, the disk still didn't work.… That afternoon, I went back to my dependable typewriter. My writing flowed. Now that is grace!

I am thankful that even when I don't understand the Lord or his ways (just like I don't understand the Internet), I can still depend on him by faith. When computers, calendars, and clocks seem to get the best of me and my time, I rely on the One who never changes. I figure God put me on earth to accomplish a certain number of things (right now I'm so far behind, I'll never die), but God is my hiding place from the tyranny of the urgent. Because of his grace, I can luxuriate in knowledge that all is well—even when the bits and bytes of my life look like scrambled gobbledygook.

The apostle Paul reminds us that through Christ, "we have gained access by faith into this grace in which we now stand" (Romans 5:2). Like the Internet superhighway, we have access to grace at any time of day or night. This grace connects us with God himself and with people worldwide who have signed on to follow him. By faith we hyperlink to the wisdom we need to live by his kingdom principles. His extravagant grace is available in a fraction of the time it takes to go through the red tape of the Department of Human Services.

What is it you need today? Remember that you have immediate access to God's Riches At Christ's Expense (GRACE). It's all right there, waiting for you to dial in. Jesus said, "God's kingdom is within you." Click on that!

The Pinson Mounds
John William Smith

It was Friday night. I had been to Jackson, Tennessee, with my date and was now returning to the college we attended in Henderson. As we approached the thriving metropolis of Pinson—a city of seventy-five souls, known worldwide for the *Pinson Mounds* (nothing to do with candy bars)—the car started pulling radically to the left, which could only mean one thing—another flat tire. Incidentally, the Pinson Mounds are some rather nondescript small hills—heaps of earth—theoretically created by some aboriginal tribesmen during the sabre-toothed tiger era—with either burial, ceremonial, or religious connotations. I swerved quickly into a little roadside pullout sheltered by oak trees.

No, the pullout wasn't such a bad place, especially in view of who I was with, and I was never one to cast aside lightly what had obviously been made available to me providentially. But eventually, I knew I was going to have to do something. Joan was very understanding, but she had to be back in the dormitory by 10:30, or we would both have to stand trial before the D.C.—Discipline Committee—to explain our whereabouts on the night in question. I had already had the dubious honor, if not pleasure, of receiving a personal invitation to appear before this venerated and august group of sages on several previous occasions and had no desire for a return engagement.

Across the street from the pullout was a one-stall, combination repair shop, junk dealer, post office, hardware, gas station, *you-name-it-we-got-it* place. It had closed before dark, but the owner/proprietor's house was next door. It was my only hope. There were no lights on, and it was obvious that they were in bed. I knocked timidly at first, but getting no response and being rather desperate, I banged loudly. This aroused the dog, who, from the sound he made, must have resembled King Kong, but he was chained. I began to hear the angry mutterings and rumblings of someone who obviously had a deep resentment toward this unwarranted disruption of his nocturnal bliss.

A light went on, the door opened slightly, and then he appeared. His hair was disheveled, his pants, hastily thrown on over long-handled underwear—which also served as his nighttime attire—hung by one suspender. He was barefoot, his eyes were half-open, and when he opened the door, he had a most unpleasant expression on his face.

"Good evening sir," I said in my most cheerful, polite, and deferential tone.

"Good *morning* you mean," he said—neither cheerfully, politely, nor deferentially. "It's got to be after midnight—Whadayawant?"

"I'm very sorry to inconvenience you, sir, but you see, I have a problem."

"Don't give me that *inconvenience* rubbish—everybody's got problems, Sonny—even me," he said as he looked sourly and suspiciously at me.

"Oh really?" I said. "I'm sorry to hear that, but you see, I have a flat tire."

"Come back tomorrow." He started to close the door.

"But I can't do that," desperation was edging into my voice. "I'm from Freed-Hardeman, over in Henderson, and my girl has to be in the dorm by 10:30, and if I don't get her there, we'll be in big trouble." I tried to slide my foot forward so he couldn't close the door.

"Put your spare tire on."

"Well sir, that's another problem. I don't *exactly* have a spare tire."

He emitted a long sigh of resignation and hopelessness, the kind of sigh that every parent learns all too quickly.

"Where's your car, Sonny?"

"Right over there behind those oaks," I said, as I pointed across the road.

"Okay. You go get the tire off and bring it over, and I'll fix it."

"Yes sir," I said enthusiastically. "But—well—actually, you see, I don't *exactly* have a jack either."

"Don't *exactly* have a jack? Son, either you have a jack or you don't have a jack. What *exactly* do you have? Do you have one *approximately?* Oh, forget it. There's one in that shed there beside the shop. Don't let Old Walt scare you; he's chained up. He sounds real fierce, but he's never *exactly* hurt anybody—seriously."

"Say, thanks a lot. You—uh—you wouldn't happen to have a lug wrench would you?"

"Oh Lord, why me?" he muttered under his breath. "Yea, there should be one in there with the jack," he said out loud. "Anything else you don't *exactly* have?"

"No sir," I said confidently, "that ought to just about do it."

It turned out that the jack was just about a foot from the end of Old Walt's chain, which looked very fragile. Old Walt was a bit much. He looked like a cross between a grizzly bear and a mountain lion, and he acted like he hadn't eaten in six weeks. He absolutely terrified me—lunging so hard against the end of his chain that he actually dragged his house, to which the chain was attached, behind him. His snarl began somewhere in the pit of his stomach, and by the time it came ripping, hissing, rattling, and roaring out his throat, it sounded like an avalanche. His eyes looked like laser beams, he had foam around his mouth, saliva dripped from his jaws, and when he snapped and ground his huge teeth, sparks flew. Old Walt was the original and archetypal *Junk Yard Dog.* I found a piece of rope, lassoed the jack, and dragged it close enough to me that I could grab it and run.

As I took the lug nuts off, I placed them in the hubcap for safe keeping. It was totally dark where the car was, and I had been too ashamed to ask for a flashlight, which I didn't *exactly* have either. The rim was rusted tightly to the drum, and I had to kick it with all my might to break it loose. When it finally flew off, it hit the edge of the hubcap and scattered the lug nuts in every direction, mostly under the car. I could only find one because the ground was about three inches

His eyes looked like laser beams, he had foam around his huge teeth, sparks flew. and when he snapped and ground his huge teeth, sparks flew.

deep in oak leaves. To make matters worse, I also discovered that I could *see through* my tire. It was absolutely ruined, and so was the inner tube. When I crossed the road again, tire in hand, I was simply wretched. My benefactor was in the garage.

"I don't think this tire is any good," I said apologetically. "You don't *happen* to have one do you?"

"I don't *happen* to have nothin', Sonny. What I got here I got *on purpose,* and I do have one." He rummaged around and eventually found a pretty decent tire.

"I could let you have this one for five bucks."

"Do you have one any less expensive? I don't *exactly* have five dollars," I said.

"How *much* less expensive? Maybe I could let it go for three," he said.

"I don't *exactly* have three either."

"Well, how much *exactly* do you have?" he said with exasperation.

"Well, if you put it in *exact* terms," I reached in my front pocket and counted out the change, "I have thirty-five cents," I said hopefully.

At that very moment, Joan appeared. She had grown tired of waiting and had come to see if I was making any progress.

Joan was very, very pretty.

"Who in the world is this?" he said, with a whistle and obvious admiration in his voice.

"Oh, this is Joan; she's my date."

He looked appreciatively at Joan.

"You sure must be some *talker,* Sonny. She sure didn't go with you for your *looks,* your *money,* your *brains,* or your *car.*"

A pretty girl does wonders to men. His whole attitude

changed in Joan's presence. He became gracious, kind, even cheerful—he forgot his inconvenience. He *gave* me the tire, found a tube, patched it, found some spare lug nuts, and helped me put it on. He even invited me to stop by and visit with him on my next trip to Jackson—if I brought Joan.

He smiled when I told him I would try to repay him some day. "Oh," he said, "That's okay. Forget it. I'll get more than my money's worth telling this story over the next twenty-five years. But nobody will believe it."

It wasn't until I got back to my room that I began to realize that I had just learned something about salvation by grace. I had learned what it means to be totally helpless, to have absolutely nothing in your hands but your need, and to receive a gift that is offered to you cheerfully and at personal cost, a gift that you can never repay.

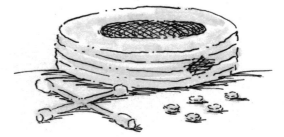

Dressed to Kill

Patsy Clairmont

Today my husband, Les, and I lunched at a charming French café. It was a delicious day, the kind you want to go on forever. The weather was perfect with enough warmth to sizzle and enough breeze to soothe. The food was scrumptious, and our table was situated outside under a wide striped awning. Music danced among the patrons, encircling us with cheery French sentiments. We drank in our surroundings of mountains in the distance, palm trees, and people nearby. Les and I chatted casually while we applauded the flaky French pastries and mused over the birds that dined on crumbs at our feet. We were delighted with the Paris ambiance, and we were pleased with each other.

Eventually, I decided to walk down the street to visit a couple of my favorite gift shops. (I have several in each city and in each state of the Union.) Les agreed to meet me in about thirty minutes at a certain store.

As I made my way to one of "my" shops, I realized the temperature was rising. The material of my beige outfit was a little weighty, and I was feeling the heat.

Then something caught my eye: a display of cool summer outfits surrounded by snappy accessories. The next thing I knew I had drifted inside and was trying them on. Wouldn't you know it? I looked darling. In fact, I was so cute I had the saleswoman clip all the tags off the outfit so I could wear it out the door. I then spotted a chipper yellow hat that would just top off the look, so I added it to the bill.

As I passed other store windows on my way to meet my husband, I caught sight of my new reflection and giggled, imagining Les's reaction.

I sashayed into the store and spotted Les chatting with the owner. Les glanced in my direction and started to turn away when something told him to look again. His head swiveled back and, as he took another gander, an incredulous look galloped across his face as he realized I was his beloved lunch date, the woman he thought he knew.

Oh, did I fail to mention that the outfit's screaming vibrancy made me look like an escapee from Ringling Brothers? Either that or I had bumped into a nauseated clown. Also, I don't wear hats.

Isn't that what happens so often in relationships? Just when we think we have someone figured out, she changes. Change is often startling, even scary. Yet many times, it's good. Change can be confusing, too. We think, *Why would anyone change when everything seemed to be going so well?* And change is usually jarring. I think change takes grace for all involved, because even the most positive kinds of change, uh, change things.

I remember when I first made a personal commitment to Christ, my decision changed me in many ways. While most of those changes pleased my husband, some of my new behaviors and beliefs annoyed him. Suddenly I didn't appreciate Les's colorful humor, and he didn't appreciate my judgmental attitude. I didn't like his beer (and all it represented), and he didn't like my control issues. I stopped smoking and decided he should, too. He decided I should mind my own business.

I desperately needed God's grace for my deficient life, and I needed to experience grace to know how to extend it to others—like my beloved husband. When a person changes, it takes time for those around her to adjust and figure out what that means to their relationship. We complicate the adjustment to our change when we insist on trying to take everyone with us. Truth is, we can't change other people; only God can do that.

We can, though, extend grace to them. Grace is the space that allows others to grow or not grow, to agree or disagree, to change or remain unchanged. No wonder grace is a gift from God; left on our own, we humans just don't have that kind of spacious room inside us.

When we understand the great value in grace, then even when those around us show up dressed to kill, we won't. Instead, we will share the gift that God has so graciously bestowed upon us.

Source Notes

Chapter 1: humoR for the spirit

"Hey, Kids, Wanna Ride?" taken from *Laugh Again*, Charles R. Swindoll, copyright © 1991, Word Publishing, Nashville, Tennessee. All rights reserved. Used by permission.

"You Gotta Hold the Baby Even When She Spits" reprinted from *At the Corner of Mundane and Grace*. Copyright © 1999 by Chris Fabry. Used by permission of WaterBrook Press, Colorado Springs, CO. All rights reserved.

"Getting Little" taken from *Lightposts for Living* by Thomas Kinkade. Copyright © 1999 by Media Arts Group, Inc. By permission of Warner Books, Inc.

"Remembering What to Forget" reprinted from *I'm Trying to Number My Days, But I Keep Losing Count!* Copyright © 1998 by Al Sanders. Used by permission of WaterBrook Press, Colorado Springs, CO. All rights reserved.

Chapter 2: the gift of humoR

"You Did This for Me?" taken from *He Chose the Nails*, Max Lucado, copyright © 2000, Word Publishing, Nashville, Tennessee. All rights reserved. Used by permission.

"How to Buy Gifts for Dummies" taken from *Chonda Pierce on Her Soapbox* by Chonda Pierce. Copyright © 1999 by Chonda Pierce. Used by permission of Zondervan Publishing House.

"The Gift" taken from *Save Me, I Fell in the Carpool* by Nancy Moser. Copyright © 1997. Used by permission.

"Flowers and Weeds" excerpted from *Home Town Tales*, © 1998, by Philip Gulley. Used by permission of Multnomah Publishers, Inc.

Chapter 3: humoR on the homefront

"Encroaching the Throne" taken from *The Lord Is My Shepherd and I'm About to be Sheared* by G. Ron Darbee. Copyright © 1998. Used by permission, Broadman & Holman Publishers.

"Cleanliness Is Next to Godliness" taken from *Happily Ever After...and 21 Other Myths about Family Life* by Karen Scalf Linamen. Copyright © 1997. Used by permission, Fleming H. Revell, a division of Baker Book House Company.

"Potty Talk for the Romantically Inclined" taken from *Mama Said There'd Be Days like This* by Charlene Ann Baumbich. Copyright © 1995. Used by permission.

"Kitchen Hall of Fame" by Marti Attoun. This article first appeared in *Christian Parenting Today* magazine (November/ December 1994), a publication of Christianity Today, Inc. Used by permission.

Chapter 4: dad—the family comedian

"Of Fathers and Children" taken from *I Wonder What Noah Did with the Woodpeckers* by Tim Wildmon. Copyright © 1998. Used by permission, Promise Press, an imprint of Barbour Publishing.

"Ripped Seams and Baby's Screams" reprinted from *At the Corner of*

Mundane and Grace. Copyright © 1999 by Chris Fabry. Used by permission of WaterBrook Press, Colorado Springs, CO. All rights reserved.

"King of the Mountain" by Harold B. Smith. This article first appeared in *Christian Parenting Today* magazine (May/June 1998), a publication of Christianity Today, Inc. Used by permission.

"The Game of Life" taken from *The Lord Is My Shepherd and I'm About to Be Sheared* by G. Ron Darbee. Copyright © 1998. Used by permission, Broadman & Holman Publishers.

Chapter 5: merriment for moms

"The ABCs of Mommyhood" by Nancy Kennedy. This article first appeared in *Christian Parenting Today* magazine (January/February 1995), a publication of Christianity Today, Inc. Used by permission.

"Excuse Me?" by Marti Attoun. This article first appeared in *Christian Parenting Today* magazine (July/August 1994), a publication of Christianity Today, Inc. Used by permission.

"Is It Real, or Is It Just Mucus?" taken from *Mama Said There'd Be Days like This* by Charlene Ann Baumbich. Copyright © 1995. Used by permission.

"Get on Board That Potty Train" taken from *Mom on the Run* by Nancy Kennedy. Copyright © 1996. Used by permission.

Chapter 6: good sports—laughter on the playing field

"Has Anyone Seen My Husband's Camouflage?" taken from *Chonda Pierce on Her Soapbox* by Chonda Pierce. Copyright © 1999 by Chonda Pierce. Used by permission of Zondervan Publishing House.

"Hanging Up the High Tops" by Jim Killam. This article first appeared in *Marriage Partnership* magazine (Fall 1999), a publication of Christianity Today, Inc. Used by permission.

"Can't Beat Fun at the Old Ballpark (Although Our Boys Have Tried)" by Lynn Bowen Walker. This article first appeared in *Marriage Partnership* magazine (Spring 1992), a publication of Christianity Today, Inc. Used by permission.

"It's All Downhill from Here" taken from *Lighten Up!* by Ken Davis. Copyright © 2000 by Ken Davis. Used by permission of Zondervan Publishing House.

Chapter 7: viva la difference— humoR between men and women

"Hurry Up, We're Going to Be Late" taken from *Women Are Always Right and Men Are Never Wrong,* Joey O'Connor, copyright © 1998, Word Publishing, Nashville, Tennessee. All rights reserved. Used by permission.

"The Upchuck That Saved Our Marriage" taken from *Mama Said There'd Be Days like This* by Charlene Ann Baumbich. Copyright © 1995. Used by permission.

"He Tarzan, Me Jane. We Friends?" taken from *Chocolate Chili Pepper Love.* Copyright © 2000 by Becky Freeman. Published by Harvest House Publishers, Eugene, Oregon 97402. Used by Permission.

"Love Must Be Show-and-Tell" taken from *I Wonder What Noah Did with the Woodpeckers?* by Tim Wildmon. Copyright © 1998. Used by permission, Promise Press, an imprint of Barbour Publishing.

Chapter 8: it's my body and i'll cry if i want to— weighty humor

"Absolutely Flabulous" taken from *Lighten Up!* by Ken Davis. Copyright © 2000 by Ken Davis. Used by permission of Zondervan Publishing House.

"Ol' Blue Eyes" taken from *Wide My World, Narrow My Bed* by Luci Swindoll. Copyright © 1982. Used by permission.

"Rejoice!" by Sheila Walsh taken from *Extravagant Grace* by Patsy Clairmont, Barbara E. Johnson, Marilyn Meberg, Luci Swindoll, Sheila Walsh, and Thelma Wells. Copyright © 2000 by Women of Faith, Inc. Used by permission of Zondervan Publishing House.

"Do Plastic Surgeons Take Visa?" taken from *Do Plastic Surgeons Take Visa?,* Kathy Peel, copyright © 1992, Word Publishing, Nashville, Tennessee. All rights reserved. Used by permission.

Chapter 9: the family that laughs together...

"Vulcan Child Care" by Dan N. "Max" Mayhew. Copyright © 1998 Max Features. This article first appeared in *Portland Family Magazine* (January 1999). Used by permission.

"Tuning In" taken from *Save Me, I Fell in the Carpool* by Nancy Moser. Copyright © 1997. Used by permission.

"The Toni" taken from *Swan's Soup and Salad* by Dr. Dennis Swanberg. Copyright © 1999. Used by permission, Howard Publishing Company.

"Teen Hair Disaster" by Dan N. "Max" Mayhew. Copyright © 1998 Max Features. This article first appeared in *Portland Family Magazine* (October 1998). Used by permission.

Chapter 10: amusing animals—pet humor

"Experiencing Dog" reprinted from *At the Corner of Mundane and Grace*. Copyright © 1999 by Chris Fabry. Used by permission of WaterBrook Press, Colorado Springs, CO. All rights reserved.

"Chippie Doesn't Sing Much Anymore" taken from *Never Lick a Moving Blender!* by Marvin Phillips. Copyright © 1996. Used by permission, Howard Publishing Company.

"Pet Peeves" taken from *An Owner's Guide to Fatherhood* by Chris Ewing. Copyright © 2000. Used by permission, Promise Press, an imprint of Barbour Publishing.

"Princess Fur-Face" by Marilyn Meberg taken from *Extravagant Grace* by Patsy Clairmont, Barbara E. Johnson, Marilyn Meberg, Luci Swindoll, Sheila Walsh, and Thelma Wells. Copyright © 2000 by Women of Faith, Inc. Used by permission of Zondervan Publishing House.

Chapter 11: love and laughter—humor in marriage

"Adam and Eve" taken from *My Mother's Favorite Song* by John William Smith. Copyright © 1995. Used by permission, Howard Publishing Company.

"Shut the Door" taken from *Dated Jekyll, Married Hyde* by Laura Jensen Walker. Copyright © 1997. Used by permission, Bethany House Publishers.

"How to Handle a Woman" taken from *Chocolate Chili Pepper Love.* Copyright © 2000 by Becky Freeman. Published by Harvest House Publishers, Eugene, Oregon 97402. Used by Permission.

"I'm Right and You're Wrong" taken from *Women Are Always Right and Men Are Never Wrong*, Joey O'Connor, copyright © 1998, Word Publishing, Nashville, Tennessee. All rights reserved. Used by permission.

Chapter 12: the funny thing about grace

"Wiped Out" taken from *God Uses Cracked Pots* by Patsy Clairmont, a Focus on the Family book published by Tyndale House Publishers. Copyright © 1991 by Patsy Clairmont. All rights reserved. International copyright secured. Used by permission.

"God's E-mail" by Barbara Johnson taken from *Extravagant Grace* by Patsy Clairmont, Barbara E. Johnson, Marilyn Meberg, Luci Swindoll, Sheila Walsh, and Thelma Wells. Copyright © 2000 by Women of Faith, Inc. Used by permission of Zondervan Publishing House.

"The Pinson Mounds" taken from *My Mother's Favorite Song* by John William Smith. Copyright © 1995. Used by permission, Howard Publishing Company.

"Dressed to Kill" by Patsy Clairmont taken from *Extravagant Grace* by Patsy Clairmont, Barbara E. Johnson, Marilyn Meberg, Luci Swindoll, Sheila Walsh, and Thelma Wells. Copyright © 2000 by Women of Faith, Inc. Used by permission of Zondervan Publishing House.

C♥ntribut♥rs

Marti Attoun, mother of three, is a retired newspaper columnist and freelance writer living in Joplin, Missouri.

Charlene Baumbich is an author, speaker, and humorist who invites readers to drop by www.dontmissyourlife.com to visit. She lives in Glen Ellyn, Illinois, with her husband, George.

Patsy Clairmont, a featured speaker at Women of Faith conferences, is the author of numerous best-selling books, including *I Love Being a Woman* and *Sportin' a 'Tude*. She makes her home in Brighton, Michigan.

G. Ron Darbee is the author of *Wrestling for Remote Control* and *The Lord Is My Shepherd and I'm About to Be Sheared!*

Ken Davis is a highly sought-after speaker who has addressed such diverse groups as the Gaither Praise Gathering, The Kellogg Corporation, and Focus on the Family with his unique blend of humor and inspiration. His daily radio program, *Lighten Up!* is broadcast on more than 500 stations nationwide.

Chris Ewing is the author of *An Owner's Guide to Fatherhood: Living with Children and Other Creatures.* He has been married for more than two decades and is the father of three children.

contributors

Chris Fabry, a popular writer, broadcaster, and speaker, lives near Chicago with his wife and seven children. The former host of Moody Broadcasting's *Open Line* program, he is now heard daily on *Love Worth Finding* with Adrian Rogers. His books include *At the Corner of Mundane and Grace* and *The H.I.M. Book*.

Becky Freeman is the best-selling author of *Worms in My Tea* and *Real Magnolias*. Her "Marriage 911" column appears regularly in *Home Life* magazine. She is also an in-demand speaker. She and her husband, Scott, live in Greenville, Texas, with their four children.

Philip Gulley, a Quaker minister from Danville, Indiana, is the author of *Front Porch Tales* and *Home Town Tales*. He and his wife, Joan, are the parents of two sons.

Barbara Johnson is the author of many best-selling books of humor and inspiration, including *Boomerang Joy* and *Stick a Geranium in Your Hat and Be Happy!* She is also a featured speaker at Women of Faith conferences. Barbara lives in La Habra, California.

Nancy Kennedy is the author of numerous books of humor and inspiration, including *Prayers God Always Answers* and *Mom on the Run*. Her articles have appeared in numerous publications, such as *Christian Parenting Today*. She and her husband, Barry, the parents of two daughters, live in Inverness, Florida.

Jim Killam teaches journalism at Northern Illinois University. He and his wife, Lauren, live in Rockford, Illinois, with their three children.

Thomas Kinkade, the highly celebrated painter, is also the author of *Lightposts for Living*. He and his wife, Nanette, live with their four daughters in northern California.

Karen Scalf Linamen is the author of numerous books, including *Pillow Talk* and *Happily Ever After*. Two of her titles have been finalists for the ECPA Gold Medallion Award. Linamen, a contributing editor for *Today's Christian Woman* magazine and the author of more than one hundred magazine articles, speaks frequently at churches, women's retreats, and writers' conferences.

Max Lucado is a minister, author, and the daily speaker of the radio program *UpWords*. His books include *In the Grip of Grace* and *The Applause of Heaven*. He and his wife, Denalyn, live in San Antonio with their three daughters.

Dan N. "Max" Mayhew is a minister, freelance writer, and a former high school teacher. His—mostly humorous—writing appears regularly in several Northwest publications. The Mayhews live in Portland, Oregon, near several households among The Summit Fellowships, a home-church community.

Marilyn Meberg, a popular Women of Faith conference speaker, is the author of numerous titles including the best-selling *I'd Rather Be Laughing* and *Choosing the Amusing.* She lives in Palm Desert, California.

Nancy Moser is the author of three books of inspirational humor and the Christian novels *The Invitation, The Quest,* and *The Temptation.*

Joey O'Connor is a popular conference speaker and the author of ten books for couples, parents, and young adults. He and his wife live in San Clemente, California, with their three children.

Kathy Peel is the author of numerous titles, including *Do Plastic Surgeons Take Visa?* and *Be Your Best: The Family Manager's Guide to Personal Success.* She is a sought-after speaker at conferences and conventions, the founder and president of Family Manager, Inc., and a staff member at *Family Circle* and *Sesame Street Parents* magazines. She and her husband, Bill, live in Dallas, Texas, and are the parents of three sons.

Marvin Phillips is a conference speaker and the author of numerous titles, including *Never Lick a Moving Blender!* and *Never Lick a Frozen Flagpole!*

Chonda Pierce is a popular speaker, comedian, author, and singer. Her work includes the books *It's Always Darkest Before the Fun Comes Up* and *Chonda Pierce On Her Soapbox,* the video *Chonda Pierce on Her Soapbox,* and the music CD *Yes...and Amen.* She lives in Nashville, Tennessee.

Al Sanders has one of the most well-known and well-loved voices in Christian radio. The founder and chairman of the board of Ambassador Advertising Agency, he has served nearly thirty major radio ministries—scripting, producing, or hosting many of Christian radio's top programs, including Chuck Swindoll's *Insight for Living, BreakPoint* with Chuck Colson, *Up Words* with Max Lucado, and Jack Hayford's *Living Way.* In 1997, he was inducted into the National Religious Broadcasters Hall of Fame.

Harold B. Smith is corporate vice president of Christianity Today, Inc. He and his wife, Judy, and their two sons live in Carol Stream, Illinois.

John William Smith is the author of numerous titles, including *Hugs for Mom, Hugs for Dad, Hugs for the Hurting, Hugs for the Holidays, Hugs to Encourage and Inspire, My Mother's Favorite Song,* and *Mother Played the Piano.* He has been a minister and teacher for more than forty years.

Dr. Dennis Swanberg is the host of his own family show, *Swan's Place,* on the FamilyNet and Odyssey networks. He is also a popular guest

on Dr. James Dobson's national broadcasts. He is the author of numerous titles, including *Swan's Soup and Salad* and *Is Your Love Tank Full?*

Charles R. Swindoll is the featured speaker on the internationally broadcast radio program *Insight for Living,* the president of Dallas Theological Seminary, and the senior pastor of Stonebriar Community Church is Frisco, Texas. He and his wife, Cynthia, have four children and ten grandchildren.

Luci Swindoll, who formerly served as vice president of public relations for Insight for Living and as an executive with Mobil Oil Corp., is the author of numerous titles, including *Celebrating Life.* Luci is also one of the featured speakers at Women of Faith conferences. She resides in Palm Desert, California.

Laura Jensen Walker is a popular public speaker and author whose works include *Dated Jekyll, Married Hyde: Delighting in the Differences Between Men and Women.* She and her husband make their home in northern California.

Lynn Bowen Walker is a freelance writer whose work has appeared in numerous periodicals, including *Marriage Partnership, Christian Parenting Today, Moody, Glamour,* and *American Baby.* She holds a journalism degree from Stanford University. Lynn and her husband, Mark, live in Los Gatos, California, and are the parents of two sons.

Sheila Walsh is a popular singer, songwriter, and author whose books include *Honestly* and *Bring Back the Joy.* Her albums include *Blue Waters, Future Eyes,* and the Grammy- and Dove-award–nominated *War of Love.* She is well known as the former cohost of *The 700 Club* on the Christian Broadcasting Network and host of her own daily talk show, *Heart to Heart,* on The Family Channel. She lives in Nashville, Tennessee, with her husband, Barry, and son, Christian.

Tim Wildmon is vice president of the American Family Association, a Christian organization based in Tupelo, Mississippi. He and his wife, Alison, make their home in Saltillo, Mississippi, with their three children.